KU-301-101

5/72

STANDARD LOA

Please re'
item by

WITHDRAWN

Napier Polytechnic Library
British documents through the apet
MLan 7 05 8 10 52 165

3 8042 00033 5860

BRITISH
DOMESTIC DESIGN
THROUGH
THE AGES

uniform with this volume

ENGLISH ARCHITECTURE
THROUGH THE AGES

Secular Building

Leonora and Walter Ison

BRITISH FURNITURE
THROUGH THE AGES

Illustrated by Maureen Stafford ARCA
edited and with an introduction by
Robert Keith Middlemas

EUROPEAN INTERIOR DESIGN
THROUGH THE AGES

Anthony Sully
edited by Jeffrey Daniels

BRITISH DOMESTIC DESIGN THROUGH THE AGES

BRIAN KEOGH and MELVYN GILL

*Edited and with an introduction
by ROBERT PATTERSON, BSc., FMA.,
Curator Castle Museum, York.*

*Drawings by Brian Keogh
assisted by Patricia Gilliland
and Linda Nash*

ARTHUR BARKER LIMITED
5 Winsley Street London W1

NOTE

This volume was to have been written and illustrated by Brian Keogh and Melvyn Gill but
due to the tragic death of Brian Keogh in 1968 the threads of the work have been taken up
by the present authors. The authors are greatly indebted to PATRICIA GILLILAND for her
tremendous contribution in helping to finish the illustrations for the book.
Most of the illustrations are drawn from originals in the extensive collections in the Castle
Museum at York. Others are from objects in the Museum of English Rural Life at Reading,
the London Museum and the Guildhall Museum, and the authors are grateful for the willing
co-operation of the Directors of these institutions.

NAPIER COLLEGE OF COMMERCE AND TECHNOLOGY

AC 811 066212 /01   RC

MERCHISTON
745.4Q941 KEO

CON   FR £2.10

NAPIER COLLEGE LIBRARY SCIENCE & TECHNOLOGY

28509
7.05

Copyright © 1970 by Keogh, Warren, Gill Ltd.

All Rights Reserved. No part of the publication may be reproduced,
stored in a retrieval system, or transmitted, in any form or by any
means, electronic, mechanical, photocopying, recording or otherwise, without the prior permission of the copyright owner.

Printed in Great Britain
by Unwin Brothers Limited
Woking and London
SBN 213 76168 8

Introduction

Domestic Design through the Ages

To trace the development of domestic design is to trace the development of man himself for it is largely by the artefacts he keeps around him, and which outlive him, that we assess the qualities and character of their owner.

This is especially true of early man, but even in more recent times these intimate possessions disclose much that would otherwise remain unrecorded in written sources. The average man, though numerically in a majority, tends to remain a literary obscurity.

The field of domestic design is vast, but in the context of this volume has been confined to articles of personal use, found in the home, where they serve a purpose other than sheer decoration. This eliminates architecture and all aspects of pure art, and for convenience furniture and costume have also been excluded.

It would however be impossible to discuss the evolution of domestic design without passing reference to architecture, that mother of art, and to furniture, but these two subjects have been admirably dealt with in the appropriate volumes of this series.

Romano British (54 BC–AD 400)

It is at once strange that this account of domestic design should begin, in Roman times, with some of the highest standards of design attained in this country. The Romans brought with them an ordered economy and a remarkably high degree of civilization, but this was superimposed on the native population rather than assimilated, and the Britons occupied the role of second-class citizens.

The Romans combined fine aesthetic appreciation with a high degree of craftsmanship, and when this combination was applied to a simplicity of basic materials the result was of a very high order. The basic materials were essentially wood, pottery, bronze, and iron, with the addition of bone, glass, lead, leather and silver. The glazing of pottery was unknown, so decoration was largely textural, by incision or by application, and the fine moulded finish of the Samian ware or terra sigillata has never been surpassed. This decoration is obviously based on the silverware of the period, and it was in their silver and gold work that the Romans really excelled.

Even their textiles were exceptional and wool cloth woven at Winchester for the Emperors was so fine it was 'comparable to a spider's web'.

After the departure of the Romans from Britain around AD 420 the native population found it was incapable of maintaining the high degree of civilization. A rapid lowering of standards was inevitable, and the successive Danish and Saxon invasions led to further decline and into the depths of the Dark Ages, which lasted until the Norman conquest.

Mediaeval (*1066–1500*)

Salvation came with the arrival of the Normans in 1066, for they brought with them not only a greater awareness of design but also provided the order and security which are essential prerequisites to any cultural advance. Their ideas and styles were assimilated by the local craftsmen and successfully translated into wood, stone, pottery and metal. Gradually over the next four centuries an over-riding style evolved which for the first time could be called English, and which culminated in one of Britain's greatest contributions to architecture, the decorated Perpendicular Gothic of around 1500.

An era that produced such outstanding architecture also created similar standards of design in furniture and in smaller personal possessions, but as always it is the pottery and to a lesser extent the metal objects which tend to be preserved for subsequent generations. By their nature these objects of pottery, and of metals such as iron and bronze, tend to be local manufactures of rural origin, and are thereby outside the main stream of fashion and style. Nevertheless these designs are very satisfying and reflect the solid and purposeful character of the people, with a sureness of touch based on a complete mastery of the material by the craftsman. This was a mastery acquired by generations of craftsmen with a deep practical knowledge of their material and a great respect for its capabilities and limitations. The craftsman was his own designer.

Materials were still simple and few, but glazing had been added to pottery, and was used on the coarse earthenware of the period with great effect. The glaze was dripped in purely functional manner with accidental decorative effects, and it was this honesty of design coupled with a functional sincerity that produced such aesthetic satisfaction. This is almost a definition of good design.

The ironwork of the period was also of a high order and reflected more the Gothic architecture of the time. The wrought iron scroll-work was particularly attractive, and every hearth was a monument to the art of the blacksmith in the shape of fire dogs, spits and hooks.

The bronze skillets, cauldrons, ewers and mortars were well cast of robust design, and a sheet brass known as latten now enabled shallow bowls to be beaten out of much thinner metal and decorated by embossing. The tableware was of a high standard, and the spoons particularly attractive in design with the stems already differentiated into various styles.

Tudor to Jacobean (*1500–1700*).

Just as English craftsmen were reaching a peak in design standards they suffered a serious setback which debased their art and aspirations for more than a hundred years.

This began during the first half of the 16th Century when it became fashionable for the sons of the nobility, and of the newly prosperous merchant class, to be sent to Italy to benefit from the rebirth of knowledge and culture that was taking place. Many no doubt understood and appreciated the new development, but many more certainly did not, yet they all brought back with them visions of an 'Italianate' style. When these visions turned into grandiose schemes the craftsmen had to be instructed in the new idiom. They understood these foreign ideas even less and naturally resented and in fact despised them. They regarded it all as a mere whim, a transient fad, that would disappear as rapidly as it had been introduced.

As after the Roman occupation the craftsman was no longer the designer of his own details, and the new designer was a patron rather than a craftsman and was guided only by scanty publications and little personal understanding.

Small wonder that the craftsman produced a most unhappy marriage of Italianate columns and flimsy details on an essentially Gothic structure. This started of course with architecture and spread down the scale to furniture and personal possessions, until almost everything reflected the latest fashion.

This was a style imposed from above, by the nobility and wealthy merchants, so naturally precious articles of gold and silver were affected first and to the greatest extent, whilst more homely articles of wrought iron, bronze and pottery were affected last and least. Some of the designs of silver were so confused that they could have passed un-noticed at the Great Exhibition of 1851!

All this was the effect of the Renaissance on design in this country.

The everyday articles of pewter and glass came through this period without losing their simplicity of form and line, and the latten and brass candlesticks lagged far behind their silver counterparts, but perhaps the least affected were the textiles and tapestries. These played a very important part in the furnishing of the house, as wall hangings and as cushions, and the tapestry designs were purely English in concept – bold, unrestricted and colourful.

The Elizabethan period from 1558 to 1603 was undoubtedly one of confusion of thought, uncertainty in design and insincerity in execution, arising out of the conflict between the native Gothic and the imported Italianate styles. One of the few who succeeded in uniting these opposing schools was Inigo Jones (1573–1652) who was the first great architect and designer of the classical style in an English idiom. He successfully reunited the craftsmen with a compromise style which was acceptable to all and which allowed the traditional skills to re-emerge.

Another set-back however was soon to be occasioned by the Puritan outlook of the Cromwellian Government (1649–1660). All ornamentation was regarded as superfluous, and personal comfort as sinful. Wine glasses were for drunkards, mirrors pandered to vanity, and cushions were a luxury. In this atmosphere domestic design suffered a serious blow, especially in the applied arts, but there were many compensations, for the stripping of excess decoration was often an improvement. It permitted a return to basic form and restrained ornamentation, and provided an opportunity to view objectively the current trends.

Many of the nobility and prosperous classes left England during this period to escape the repressions of the Puritans, and this had the welcome effect of temporarily freeing the craftsmen from their patrons. This restored their confidence and pride and initiated improvements in techniques and materials. The suppression of wood carving gave greater scope to the wood turners and led to the introduction of ring and bobbin turning, knob and ball and the many varieties of spiral twist. Even the oak itself was now being augmented by the use of fruit woods, and ash, yew and walnut.

This was an age of quiet experiment and invention – cast iron was established and the clock and instrument makers prospered – and unknowingly the foundations of the Industrial Revolution were being laid.

The return of Charles II to England in 1660 was a gay occasion, and this gaiety was soon reflected in the design of almost everything. Beginning naturally with architecture and furniture design the new styles spread in all directions, but this time the styles, although still 'Italianate' in origin, were successful. The difference was that the patrons had now returned from a prolonged stay in Europe with a much better understanding of the principles involved, and the craftsmen had stripped the last vestiges of gothic decoration from their work and were in a position to accept the new ideas.

Craftsmen everywhere prospered. The goldsmith and silversmith, the pewterer, the tinsmith, the weaver, joiner, glass-blower, brass founder, blacksmith and plumber all worked in complete harmony with the new designers – the very competent architects of the time. Names like Christopher Wren (1632–1723), John Vanbrugh (1664–1726), and William Kent (1683–1748) came to the fore and led the country into the Golden Age of Design, from 1660 to 1830.

Queen Anne and Georgian (1700–1800)

The Eighteenth century was without doubt the greatest period in the history of domestic design in this country.

Significantly the names that emerge like Chippendale (1740's–1760's), Hepplewhite (1770's–1780's) and Sheraton (1790's) are furniture designers, rather than architects, and even Robert Adam (1728–1792) combined designing with his architecture, and their influence on domestic design is consequently most marked.

Many trends follow each other in fairly rapid succession during the century, each being the result of some outside influence, but each being perfectly assimilated by the designers and interpreted with understanding by the craftsmen. The obviously architectural styles of the 1680's with heavy columns, ballister turning and the favourite S-scroll soon gave way to the rounded curves and flowing lines of the Queen Anne period from 1702–14.

This in turn developed during the reign of George I (1714–1727) into an extravaganza of asymmetrical scrolls, acanthus leaves, cherubs, classical figures, lions' heads and masks of the Baroque style. About 1740 this gradually changed into a much daintier form based on swirling C and S scrolls, shells, floral motifs and festoons, and known as the Rococo from the French 'rocaille coquille' (i.e. rock and shell work). By the middle of the century this had been supplemented by an equally exuberant oriental influence, with Chinese motifs and other chinoiserie intermingling with the scrolls and quite fantastically even Gothic features were absorbed. This ability to combine all these conflicting influences in a unified and very successful design, which is at the same time characteristically English, is a measure of the confidence of the designers and of the sympathy and competence of the craftsmen of the period. This period was the natural culmination of centuries of hand craftsmanship evolving at a rate that could readily be assimilated, and without any violent fundamental changes in materials or processes.

The 1760's saw a return to much simpler outlines inspired by ancient Greece with motifs based on egg-and-dart moulding, dentils, anthemion and honeysuckle. This classic revival was led by Robert Adam and continued in fashion into the 19th century, although becoming somewhat coarser and heavier in the 1790's.

This Golden Age of Design was a period of prosperity and gracious living combined with innovation and invention, and this combination provided almost limitless opportunities for the skills of designers and craftsmen.

Tea became popular and provided new scope for silversmiths and potters to provide the necessary tableware; new articles of furniture provided more display surfaces for treasured pieces; new fashions created new demands, and the expanding prosperity increased the requirements down the social scale.

Great china and pottery factories thrived at Chelsea, Bow, Bristol, Worcester and Derby, but the greatest and most progressive of all was Josiah Wedgwood who established his first factory in Burslem in 1759 and his famous 'Etruria' works at Hanley ten years later.

Silversmiths produced their finest work during this century, and Sheffield plate, that entirely English craft of sandwiched silver and copper, was invented by Thomas Bolsover of Sheffield in 1743, and was followed by Joseph Hancock who established his factory in 1758. Painted enamels for boxes, caskets, caddies, and scent bottles were produced at Battersea in 1753 and at the Bilston and Birmingham factories a little earlier.

Glassware was supplied by the great factories at Greenwich, Bristol, Birmingham, Sunderland, Stourbridge, and Warrington, as well as the Irish glasshouses at Belfast, Dublin, Cork and Waterford.

Papier mâché was a product of this era, developed by Henry Clay of Birmingham in 1772, but whatever the material or purpose nothing was too insignificant to benefit by good proportion and design. Even the typeface designed by John Baskerville (1706–75) of Birmingham is still unsurpassed two hundred years later.

The Industrial Revolution was now well launched, and surprisingly the new factories began under conditions of ideal relationship between the industrialist, the designer and the craftsman. Quality was not impaired and standards were not lowered – it was simply that quantities were increased.

Regency and Early Victorian (1800–1850)

Although the Regency only existed from 1811 to 1820 its influence extended from 1800 to 1830 when it gradually merged into the early Victorian of 1837, and the changeover was completed by 1850.

The Regency began as a continuation of the late Georgian styles, with strictly classical themes overriding all domestic design. The Greek and Egyptian influences produced motifs of lion's-paw feet, eagles, dolphins, caryatids and animals' legs; and the rather formal shapes gradually became heavier and more practical.

In the 1830's however a new trend appeared introduced by Augustus Pugin the fanatical mediaevalist. In 1836 he published a book contrasting the noble middle ages with 'the present decay of taste' and became the leader of a Gothic Revival which had a shattering effect on domestic design in this country from which we have scarcely recovered.

The sentimental novels of Walter Scott, based on mediaeval themes and the passionate pleas of John Ruskin, guided the general public into this Romantic movement, and gradually the classical Regency style was overlaid with pseudo-Gothic ornamentation and even Rococo motifs to produce the romantic early Victorian styles up to 1850.

During this period industrialization was proceeding apace, and mechanisation was taking over many of the handcrafts, or at least assisting and speeding up the preparatory processes. It was becoming increasingly easy to produce large quantities of ornamental motifs to apply to the surface of articles of domestic use.

At the same time these factories were beginning to attract the population from rural areas into the large towns and to create an expanding middle class, and it was this newly created middle class which was demanding these romantic Gothic designs. For the first time the domestic styles had emanated from below and the new industrialists were only too eager to satisfy this increasing public demand. Designers could do little more than pander to the population and anticipate its requirements.

New techniques were introduced and old ones improved in this search for easier, quicker and more diverse processes of manufacture. The Sheffield plate industry expanded with a host of new methods for overcoming the inherent difficulties of raw edge masking, and not surprisingly true silversmiths produced those wavy edges so difficult to imitate in plate.

Papier mâché was used not only for trays but for a wide range of articles from boxes and cabinets to chairs and tables. Cast iron production expanded and was used for every conceivable, and inconceivable, purpose including rustic garden furniture and Gothic arches. Brass of a new finer alloy and better colour was cast in a multiplicity of forms including horse-brasses and copies of Georgian candlesticks. The new lamps to burn colza oil gave additional scope, whilst Nailsea glassmakers produced everything from walking sticks to bells, and paperweights to pipes.

The grand culmination of this period was the Great Exhibition of 1851 in the Crystal Palace when all the achievements of early Victorian ingenuity were proudly displayed. It was undoubtedly a technological triumph, but a monument to confusion in design.

Late Victorian (1850–1900)

The confusion of design of the 1850's resulted originally from the conflict between the current classical and Gothic themes, and it was the ease of mechanical reproduction that magnified the effect. A reaction to both these influences was initiated by William Morris in 1861 when he founded a company to produce simply designed and craftsmen built articles based on functional mediaeval originals.

He aimed to foster a respect for the 'handmade' as opposed to the 'cheap and nasty' of the 'machine made', but unfortunately his efforts had the opposite effect for they merely led the industrialists to produce imitation handmade articles with rough finishes, false adze markings on wood or impressed hammer marks on metal.

This had a disastrous effect on design in general, and the confusion of thought was now unbounded. Any number of styles were mixed in any combinations to produce articles of bewildering and incredible form

Added to this was a general love of comfort and cosiness. Comfort revolved itself into deep, shapeless upholstery, stuffy cushions and an assemblage of firescreens and footwarmers, anti-macassars, bobble-braid and plush. Cosiness was expressed in terms of an unashamed excess of ornaments of all kinds, souvenirs, knick-knacks and personal treasures, covering the walls and every horizontal surface.

The newly created problem of soot led to dark colours and heavy all-over patterns on carpets and wallpaper, and to the widespread use of glass domes to protect wax fruits and silk flowers.

The copper coal scuttle was disguised as a painted 'purdonium' to pretend the fire was replenished by a non-existent staff.

This was the new middle class asserting its position in society by emulating a romantic vision of grandeur in the past.

Ancestry was established by the new craze for collecting antique furniture in the 1870's and 80's, and this degenerated into the manufacture of quite impossible 'antiques' and into the ruinous embellishment of the genuinely old.

Not only were the Victorians lacking in standards of design or quality, but they were dangerously unaware of their limitations.

Edwardian (1900–1920)

The period from 1900 to 1920 is characteristically the Edwardian era (1901–10) extended to include the first world war and is largely homogeneous in outlook and design.

The new century opened with a revolt against the Victorian confusion of applied 'artistry' to all objects. This eastern-inspired movement became known as 'L'Art Nouveau' and aimed at a simplification of form overlaid with a uniformity of design. It took the form of an entwining growth of lotus leaves and tendrils interspersed with heart-shaped inlays and cut-outs. This new art acquired the appellation 'modern' and even 'futuristic', used in a derogatory sense and was at first resisted by the old school who demanded even more 'antique' imitations.

Salvation eventually came through the unappreciated and unrecognised medium of functional design. This trend actually began in the 19th century, and surprisingly with that most misused of all materials, cast iron, for it was in the unconscious functional designs of such articles as pillar boxes, bridges and railway equipment that the Victoriana really excelled. In Edwardian times this functional aspect continued to develop, mainly through the work of the car designers, and especially Rolls Royce. The engineers of the transport and communications undertakings were unknowingly leading a return to a British tradition in design based on sincerity and suitability for purpose and material.

William Lethaby was one of the few designers in 1913 who realized that 'machine work should show quite frankly that it is the child of the machine; it is the pretence and subterfuge of most machine-made things which make them disgusting'.

1920–1940

The First World War of 1914–18 brought a violent reaction against all established traditions and especially against the profusion of ornamentation and the overcrowding of roomspace that had characterised the late Victorian and to a slightly lesser degree the Edwardians. This reaction crystallized into a puritanical avoidance of all forms of ornament led by the elite, or *avant garde* as they liked to be known, and became associated with the work of the great artist and craftsman, Ernest Gimson.

The British Empire Exhibition of 1924 brought together the works of the leading designers of the period and perhaps for the first time industrial design was accepted by the general public in its own right, although still associated almost entirely with mechanical locomotion. The hand crafts of pottery, textiles, leather and glass were well represented, and also the intermediate machine-produced articles such as vacuum cleaners, gramophones, cooking equipment and kitchenware.

The emphasis on road and rail speed led to the 'streamlining' of domestic articles such as smoothing irons and perambulators, and this resulted in a commendable simplification of form.

Bodies like the British Institute of Industrial Art and the Design and Industries Association educated the public and had a considerable influence in directing the trends, so that by the mid 1930's it was possible to detect the re-emergence of an English tradition in design.

The rural crafts continued, unaffected by conscious design, and still produced satisfying forms of functional sincerity. Wooden bowls and buckets, peggy sticks and mouse traps changed little over the centuries.

This period begins with the Second World War of 1939–46, which once again resulted in reaction. The utility standards laid down by the government in 1941 brought an enforced austerity which cleared away all other conceptions and left the way open for new ideas. The first stirrings of the modish designers were labelled 'contemporary', and the styles tended to be as vague as the title.

The Council of Industrial Design did much to guide industry and the public towards higher standards of design, and the Festival of Britain Exhibition in 1951 mirrored the styles of the day. It was clear that the return to an English tradition was continuing, and that this time it was a return to a freedom of expression with an over-riding good taste.

The vastly extended range of materials, including plastics and other synthetics, coupled with the equally vast increase in techniques and equipment, make it impossible and undesirable to have a single, uniform style. There is every indication that the virility of the more recent years is leading to a healthy assimilation of form and design, decoration and functional efficiency. Previous fashions are being seen objectively and dispassionately and are being embodied and adapted with the same confidence and sincerity of the golden age.

There is every indication that the present freedom of thought, un-inhibited outlook and deeper understanding of the new methods and materials is leading to a wide appreciation of design in its domestic form – and appreciation is the prelude to realization.

Roman 55 BC – AD 420

1 Earthenware cooking pot, 2nd Century

2 Beaker with barbotine dotted decoration, 3rd Century

3 Beaker of New Forest ware, 4th Century

4 Multiple vase for decorative or ritual use, 3rd Century

5 Multiple vase for decorative or ritual use, 3rd Century

6 Oil jar of buffware, 2nd Century

7 Pottery narrow-necked jug, 1st Century

8 Pottery narrow-necked jug, 1st Century

9 Earthenware strainer, 2nd Century

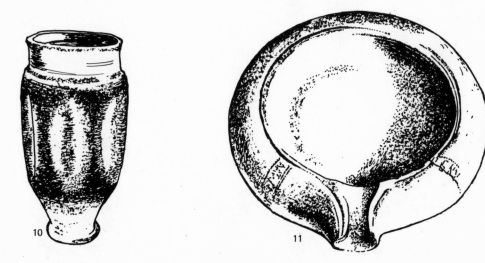

10 Indented beaker of colour-coated New Forest ware, 4th Century

11 Mortarium with gritty interior for grinding, 1st Century

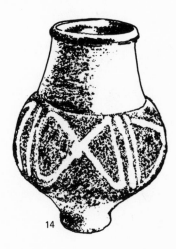

12

13

14

12 Carrot-shaped amphora for wine or oil, 1st Century

13 Castor ware beaker with barbotine scroll, 3rd Century

14 New Forest ware beaker with piped decoration, 4th Century

15 Black gloss-ware cup with barbotine decoration, 3rd Century

16 Carinated bowl with flanged rim, 1st Century

17 Brown coated jar with rouletted bands, 2nd Century

18 Buff ware jar with barbotine decoration, 1st Century

15

16

17

18

19 Samian ware or terra sigillata of fine moulded clay

20 Beaker of colour-coated Castor ware, 4th Century

21 Red burnished beaker with Anglo Saxon style decoration

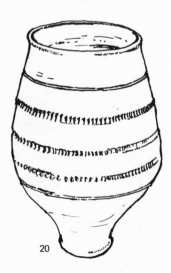

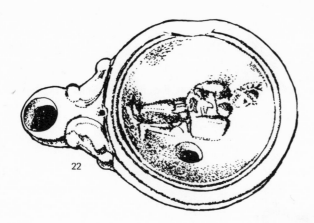

22 Pottery oil lamp, 1st Century

23 Pottery oil lamp with handle, 3rd Century

24 Bronze jug with handle ending in form of bust, 1st Century

25 Bronze oil lamp with voluted nozzles, 1st Century

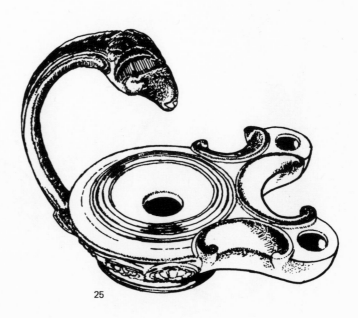

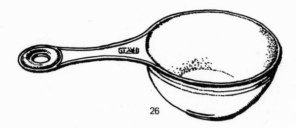

26 Bronze round-based skillet, 1st Century

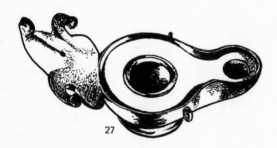

27 Bronze oil lamp with lugs for suspension, 2nd Century

28 Bronze jug with simple handle, 1st Century

29 Spherical glass flask with carrying handle

30   31   32

30 Glass flask blown into cylindrical mould,
4th Century

31 Dolphin flask for carrying oil for bathing,
2nd Century

32 Glass unguent bottle, often called a tear
bottle, 1st Century

33 Simple clay candlestick

34 Square wine jug for ease of packing

34

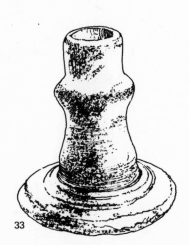

33

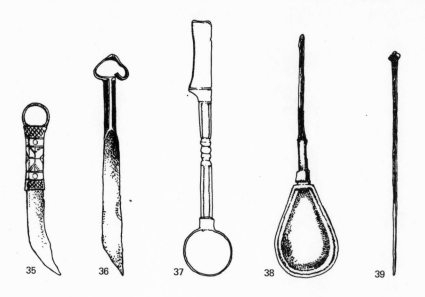

35 Bronze knife with bone grips

36 Knife without grips

37 Composite implement with blade and saw

38 Bronze fig-shaped spoon

39 Bronze skewer

40 Bronze spoon with circular bowl

41 Bronze spoon with twisted stem

42 Bronze spit or skewer

43 Knife without grips

44 Bronze knife with bone grips

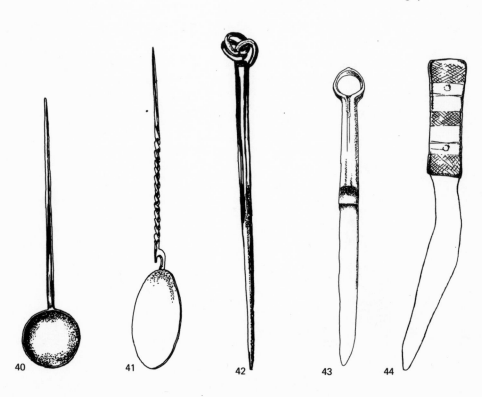

Dark Ages 420-1066

45 Saxon jar with stamped decoration, 7th Century

46 Saxon jar with stamped, combed and applied decoration, 7th Century

47 Coarse gritty jar with tubular spout, 9th Century

48 Bronze bowl with suspension lugs, 6th Century

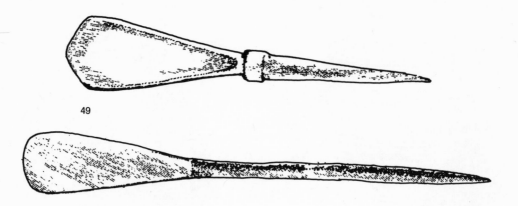

49

49 Two Saxon bone spoons, 10th Century

50 Bone hair comb, 10th Century

51 Wooden weaving comb, 10th Century

52 Three Saxon bone knife handles, 10th Century

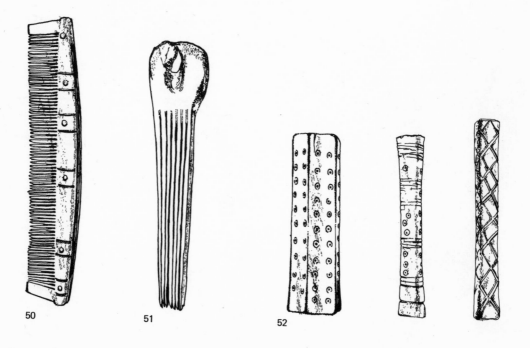

50   51   52

Mediaeval 1066–1500

53

54

53 Green glazed jug with ribbed decoration, 13th Century

54 Large decorated pitcher, 14th Century

55 Pitcher decorated in pale yellow glaze, 14th Century

56 Green glazed pitcher with pressed feet, 14th Century

56

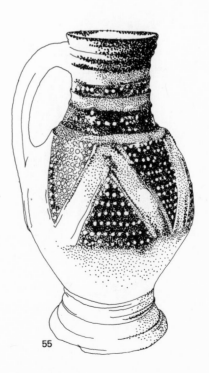

55

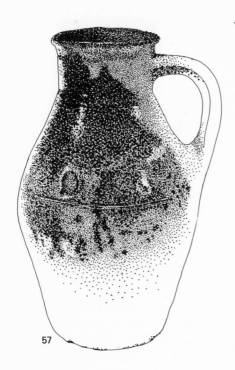

57

60

57 Brown glazed Cheam ware pitcher, 15th Century

58 Yellow glazed pitcher decorated in low relief, 14th Century

59 Pitcher with impressed decoration, 14th Century

60 Netherlands style majolica jug, 16th Century

58

59

61 Spouted pitcher with feet derived from metal ewer, 14th Century

62 Green glazed cooking pot, 13th Century

63 Brown glazed pottery measure of metal style

64 Three unglazed pottery measures

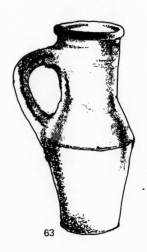

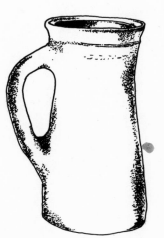

65

66

67

65 Green glazed pitcher with relief decoration, 14th Century

66 Bucket-handled vessel for heating water, 15th Century

67 Bronze jug, 14th Century

68 Multicoloured jug with parrot-beak spout, 14th Century

69 Yellow glazed pitcher with grape decoration

70 Mottled glazed jug with grotesque human mask, 14th Century

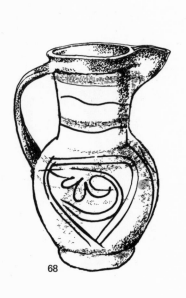

68

69

70

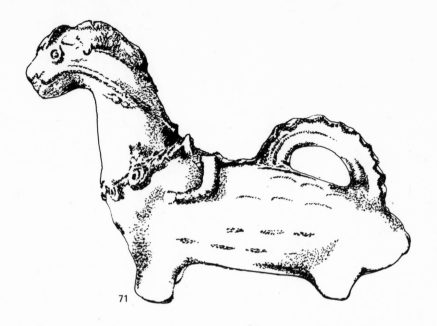

71

71 Aquamanile for hand rinsing before introduction of forks, 13th Century

72 Cresset lamp of hard grey pottery, 13th Century

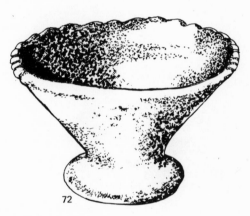

72

73 Latten (brass) bowl with burnished wavy lines, 12th Century

73

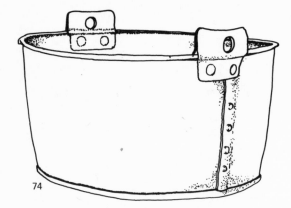

74 Bronze stewpan suspended by iron chain, 1500

75 Turned wooden bowl, 14th Century

76 Pottery pipkin with curved handle for carrying, 13th Century

77 Bronze mortar with flanges showing oriental influence

78

79

78 Cast bronze skillet

79 Bronze cauldron, 14th Century

80 Bronze ewer with Lombardic lettering, 15th Century

81 Bronze ewer with spout ending in animal's head, 15th Century

80

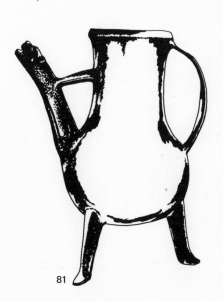

81

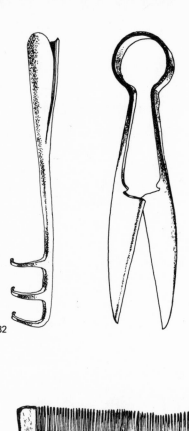
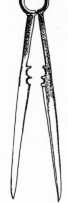

82 Flesh hook used in cooking

83 Two pairs of shears, 14th Century

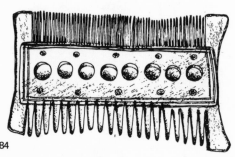

84 Bone comb with bronze plates, 14th Century

85 Hand brush or whisk of fine twigs

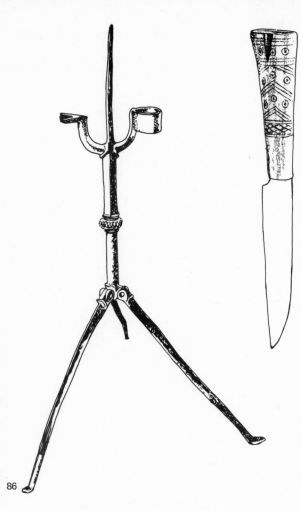

86 Bronze pricket candlestick
with folding legs

87 Two bone-handled knives,
15th Century

88 Diamond-knop spoon, 13th Century

89 Acorn knop, 13th Century

90 Modified acorn knop, 14th Century

91 Maidenhead knop, 15th Century

92 Writhen knop, 14th Century

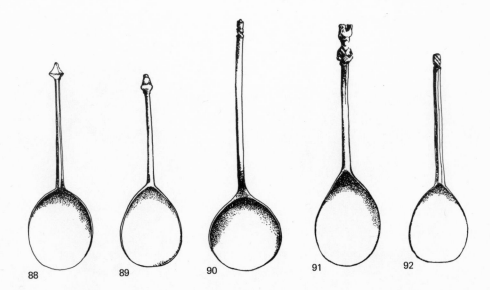

Tudor to Jacobean 1500 – 1700

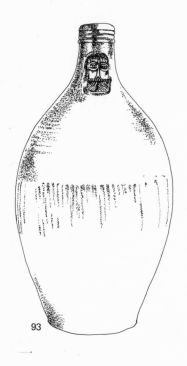

93

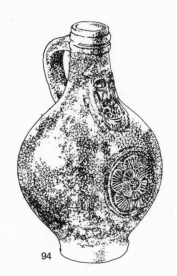

94

93 Salt-glazed stoneware wine bottle known as a Grey Beard or Bellarmine, 1650

94 Smaller stoneware Bellarmine, 1700

95 Stoneware jug with finger pressed base

96 Jug decorated with grits beneath glaze, 1650

96

95

97

98

97 Pot of blue grey glazed ware, 1690

98 Flanged pot of Metropolitan slip ware

99 Pottery pipkin of brown glazed-ware, 1650

99

100 Porringer of combed ware, 1650

101 Lambeth Delftware bowl, 1650

100

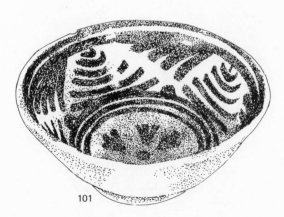

101

102

103

104

102 Blue dash charger of Lambeth Delft ware, 1675

103 Salt cellar of Metropolitan slip ware 1650

104 Slip decorated tyg with three handles and three lugs

105 Dish of Bermondes Delft ware, 1650

106 Lambeth Delft plate with Chinese style decoration. 1650

105

106

107 Beaker of stitched leather

108 Leather mug or 'Blackjack'

109 Leather costrel or harvest barrel for beer or cider

110 Large leather wine bottle

111 Wooden bottle

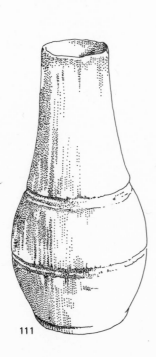

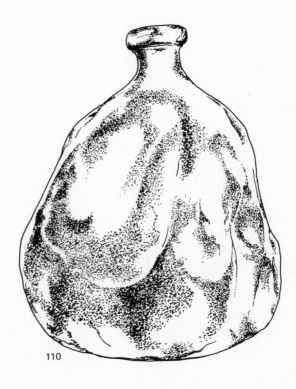

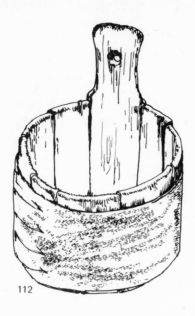

112

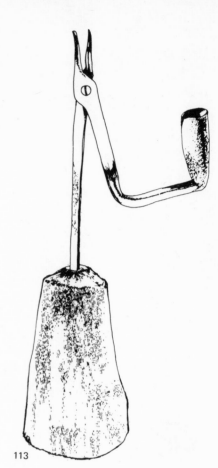

112 Wooden vessel or 'piggin' bound with hide

113 Rush light and candle holder

113

114 Pipe rack for cleaning clay pipes in fire

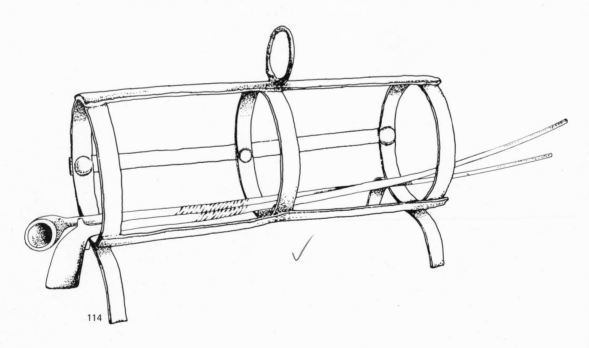

114

115

115 Pewter porringer with pierced handle

116 Brass lid of warming pan, 1620

117 Pewter plate with incised decoration

118 Pewter plate with wriggle work design

119 Pewter dish

116

119

117

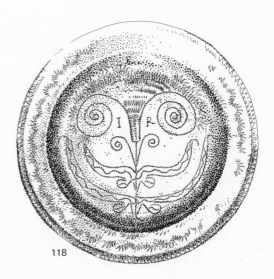

118

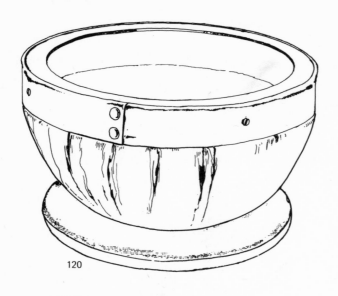

120

124

120 Walnut punch bowl with pewter lining

121 Wooden cup, originally silver mounted

122 Maplewood cup with silver mount

123 Fishmongers' silver tankard, 1672

124 Lantern-shape side-handled coffee pot

121   122   123

125 Two-handled silver cup, London 1660

126 Two-handled silver cup, York 1682

127 Two-handled pewter cup with portrait of William III, 1695

128

129

128 Brass lantern clock by Bowyer of
London, 1630

129 Square table clock by Decange of
London, 1620

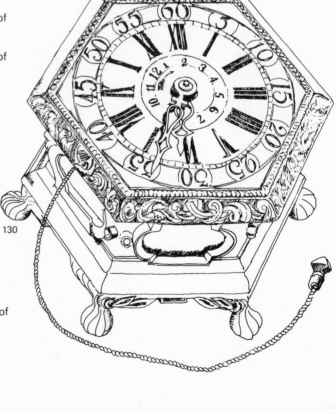

130

130 Hexagonal table clock by Ledeir of
London, 1620

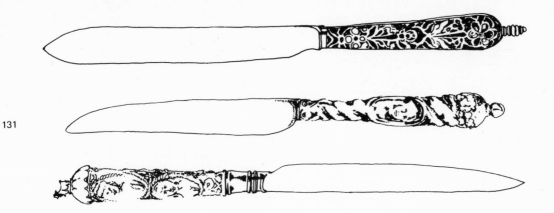

131 Knives with silver and enamel handles, 17th Century

132 Pair of table knives and sheath, 1610

133 Horn-handled knives with engraved brass butts, 16th Century

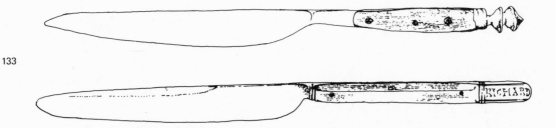

131

132

133

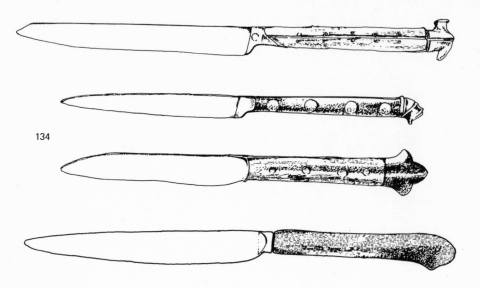

134 Wood-handled knives with brass butts as hammerhead, horse-shoe, trefoil and plain, 16th Century

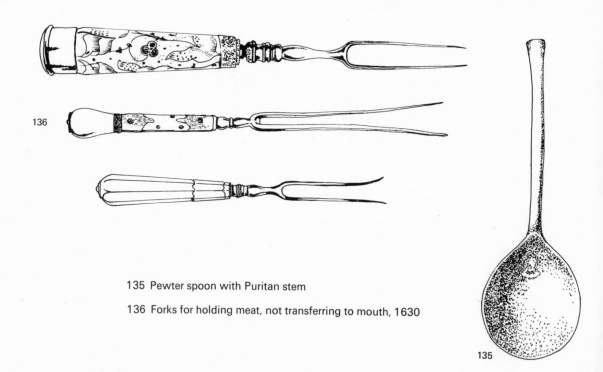

135 Pewter spoon with Puritan stem

136 Forks for holding meat, not transferring to mouth, 1630

Queen Anne and Georgian 1700–1800

137

137 Three-handled posset pot or tyg, Stafford 1707

138 Stoneware mug with moulded hunting scene, Nottingham 1770

139 Ale tankard, Worcester 1793

140 Jug with mask spout of Liverpool type, 1789

139

138

140

141 Side-handled coffee or chocolate jug

144 Astbury ware coffee pot, 1740

142 Oval teapot, Worcester 1796

145 Lowestoft teapot in Chinese style, 1787

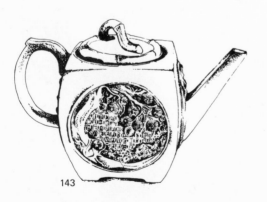

143 Teapot of caneware by Turner, 1780

146 Leeds ware teapot in Chinese style, 1800

147 Handleless teacup and saucer, Worcester

148 Handleless teacup and saucer, Stafford

149 Blue jasper ware cup and saucer, Wedgwood 1786

150 Sunderland pink lustre bowl, 1796

147

148

149

150

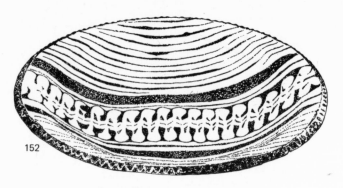

152

152 Earthenware dish with combed slip decoration, Stafford 1750

153 Polychrome Dresden style candlestick

154 Earthenware skillet with hollow handle

155 Green glaze Dutch oven dated 1727

156 Wooden platter or trencher with salt hollow

153

154

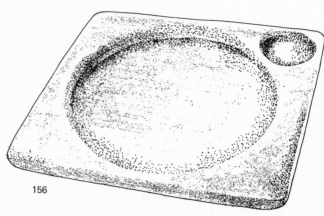

156

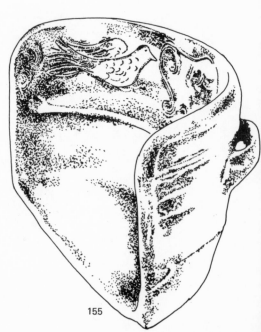

155

157

158

159

157 Wooden plate or trencher

158 Wooden porringer

159 Wooden ladle

160 Box wood powderer for glove fingers

161 Wooden casket with bur walnut lid

160

161

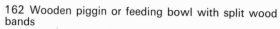
162 Wooden piggin or feeding bowl with split wood bands

162

163

163 Walnut puzzle money box

164 Set of wooden egg cups and pepper pot

165 Nesting boxwood spice boxes

164

165

167

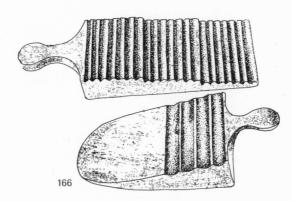

166

168

166 Mahogany plate tilters or dish slopes

167 Turned wood goblet

168 Lemon squeezer in turned boxwood

169 Punch ladle made from coconut shell

170 Mahogany wig stand

170

169

NAPIER UNIVERSITY LIBRARY

171 Skillet of cast bell metal

172 Copper ale muller with tinned interior

173 Copper kettle

174 Copper saucepan with added spout

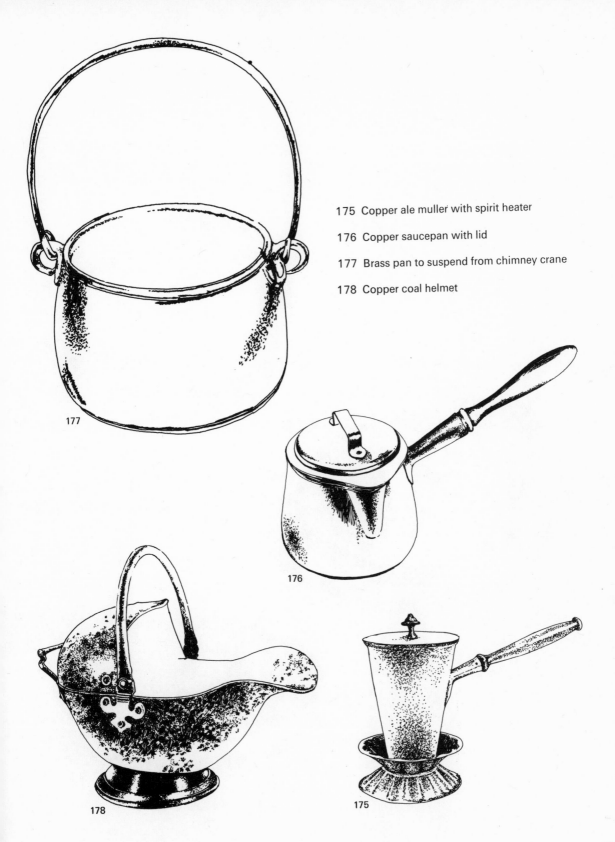

175 Copper ale muller with spirit heater

176 Copper saucepan with lid

177 Brass pan to suspend from chimney crane

178 Copper coal helmet

177

176

178

175

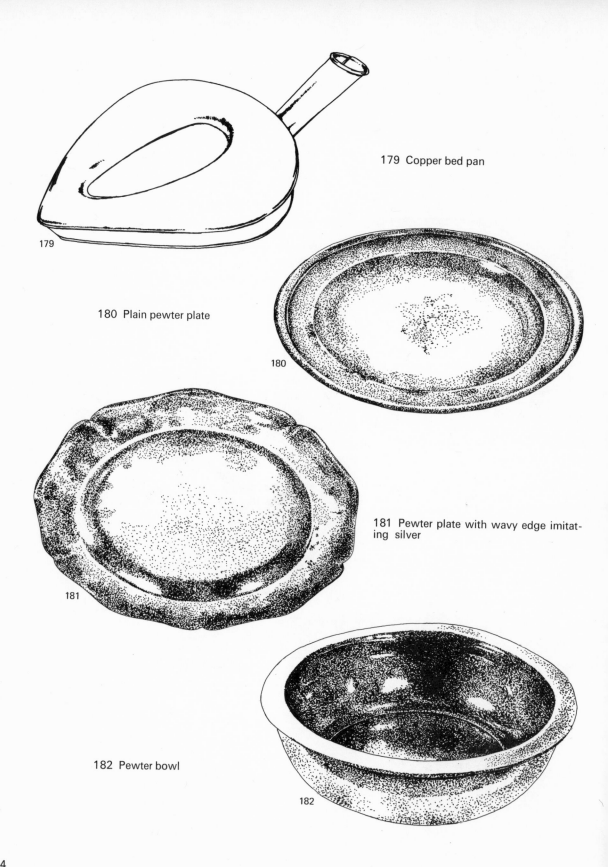

179 Copper bed pan

180 Plain pewter plate

181 Pewter plate with wavy edge imitating silver

182 Pewter bowl

183 Pewter chamber pot inscribed 'Royal Hospital'

184 Pewter bed pan

185 Pewter bread or cheese coaster

186 Iron frying pan

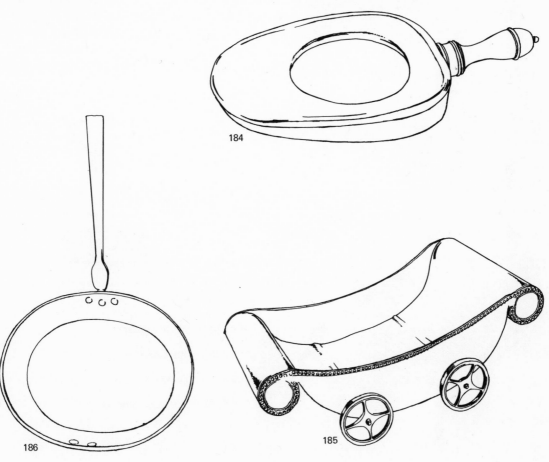

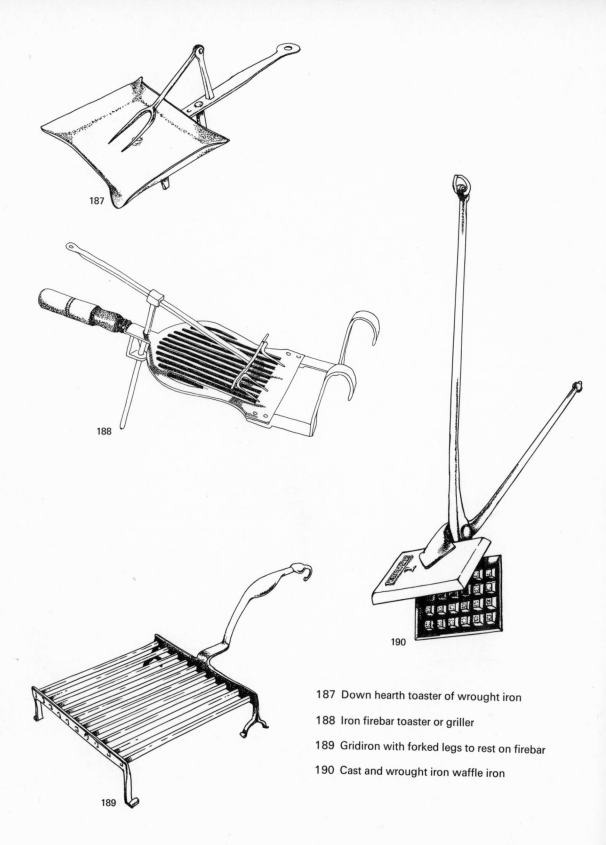

187 Down hearth toaster of wrought iron

188 Iron firebar toaster or griller

189 Gridiron with forked legs to rest on firebar

190 Cast and wrought iron waffle iron

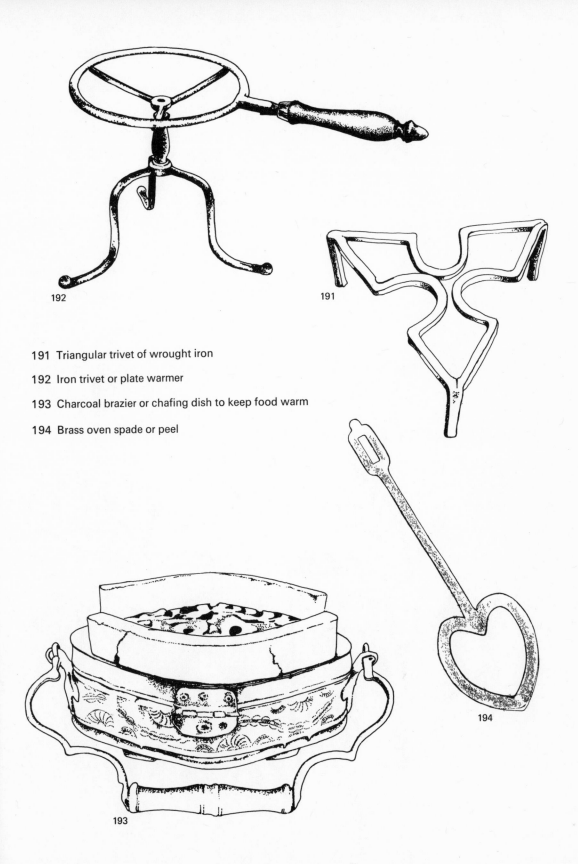

191 Triangular trivet of wrought iron

192 Iron trivet or plate warmer

193 Charcoal brazier or chafing dish to keep food warm

194 Brass oven spade or peel

195 Wooden chimney crane or reckan

196 Great wheel for spinning wool

197 Deadfall mousetrap

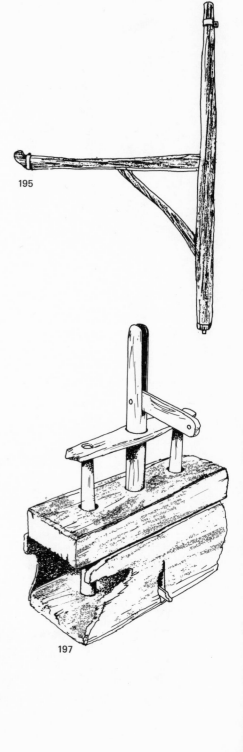

195

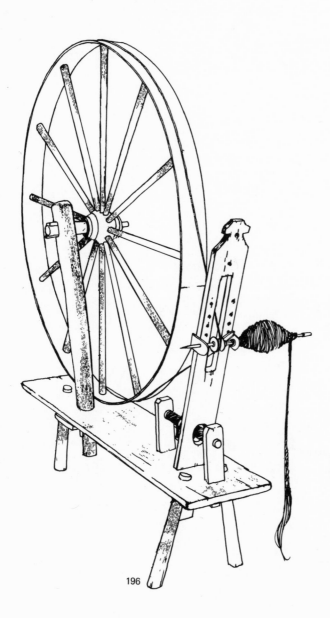

196

197

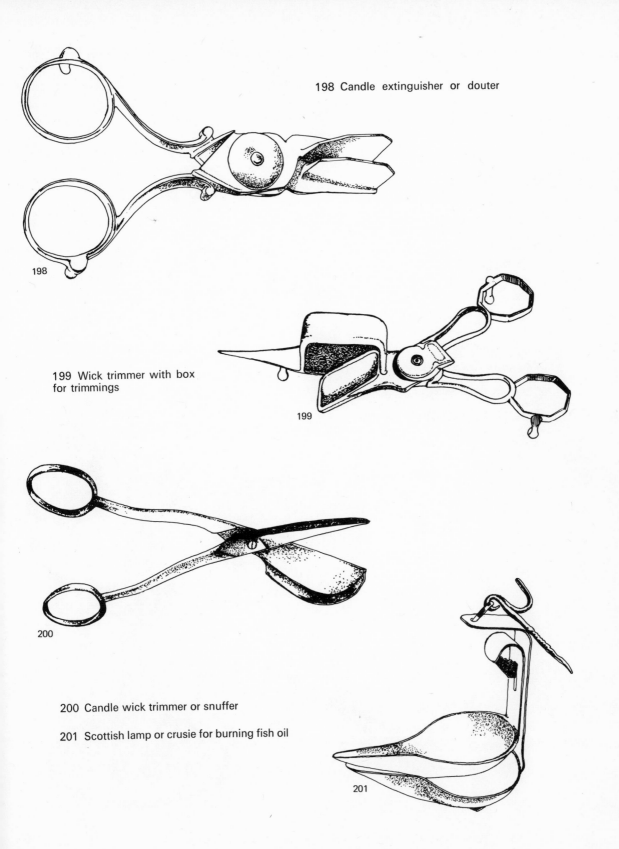

198 Candle extinguisher or douter

199 Wick trimmer with box for trimmings

200 Candle wick trimmer or snuffer

201 Scottish lamp or crusie for burning fish oil

59

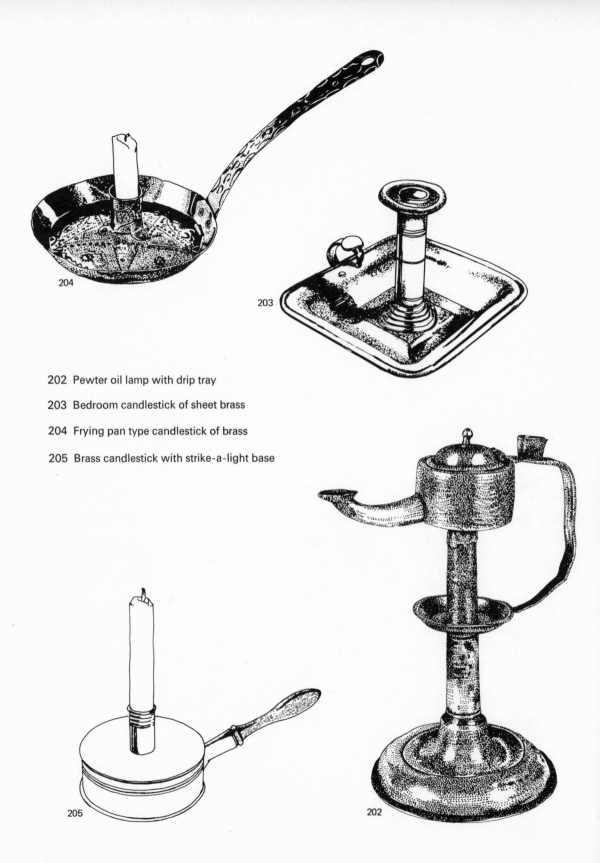

202 Pewter oil lamp with drip tray

203 Bedroom candlestick of sheet brass

204 Frying pan type candlestick of brass

205 Brass candlestick with strike-a-light base

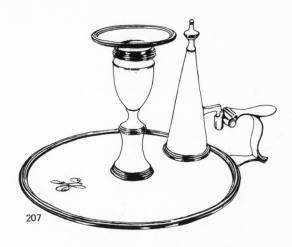

206 Bedroom candlestick with conical extinguisher, 1800

207 Silver candlestick in simple neo-classical style

208 Candlesticks of Sheffield plate in Egyptian style, 1780

209 Candelabrum of Sheffield plate

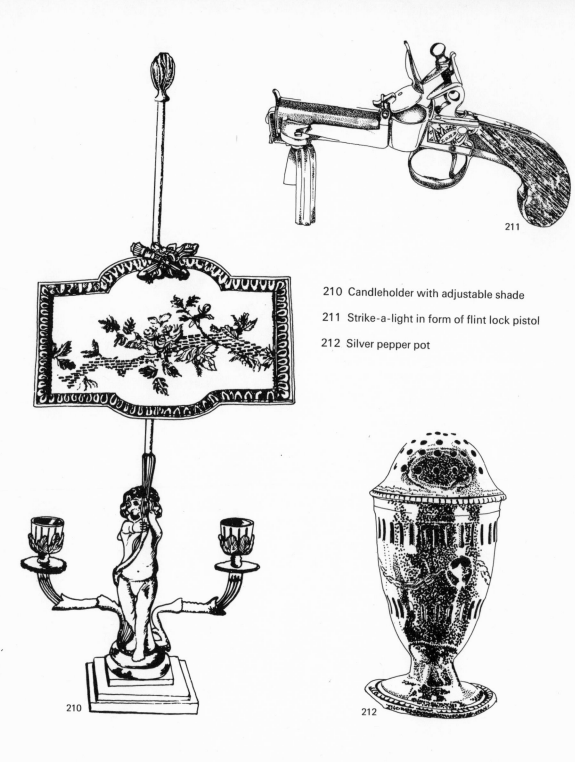

210 Candleholder with adjustable shade

211 Strike-a-light in form of flint lock pistol

212 Silver pepper pot

210

211

212

213

214

213 Silver tea caddy in bombe shape, 1750

214 Silver salt cellar

215 Sheffield plate coffee urn with spirit heater

216 Silver coffee jug in classical style, 1780

217 Silver coffee or chocolate jug, 1790

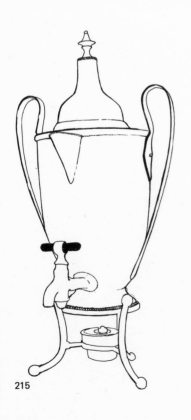

215

216

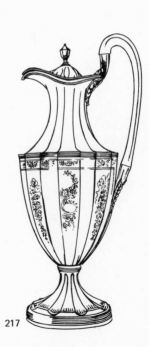

217

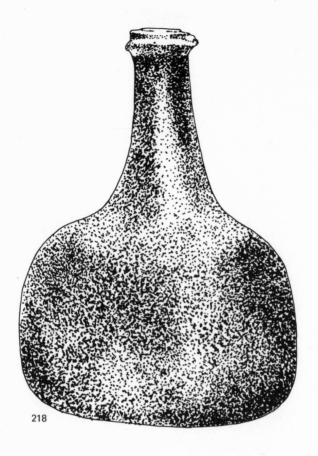

218 Green glass wine bottle

219 Rummer with plinth foot

220 Engraved glass with drawn stem

221 Wine glass with air twist stem

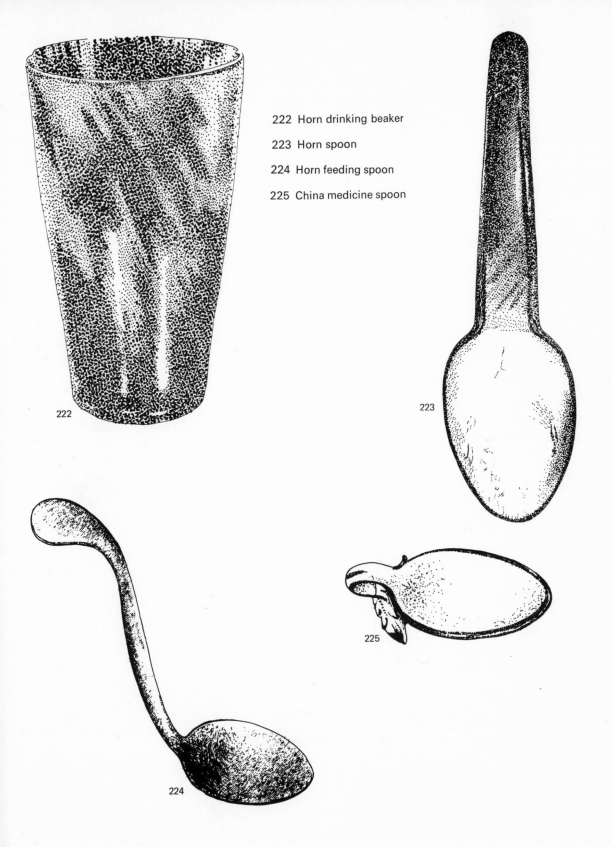

222 Horn drinking beaker

223 Horn spoon

224 Horn feeding spoon

225 China medicine spoon

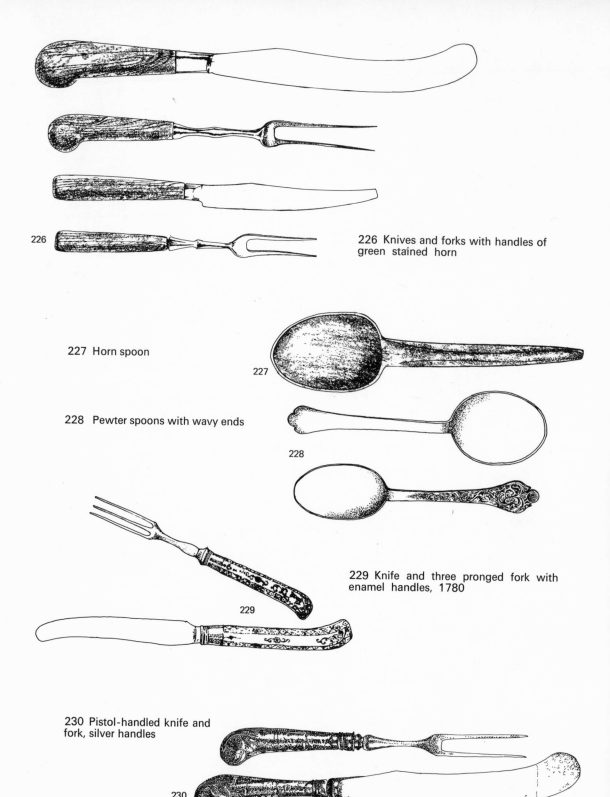

226 Knives and forks with handles of green stained horn

227 Horn spoon

228 Pewter spoons with wavy ends

229 Knife and three pronged fork with enamel handles, 1780

230 Pistol-handled knife and fork, silver handles

Regency and Early Victorian 1800 – 1850

231

232

231 Vase decorated with view of Cumberland, Bloor Derby, 1825

232 Milk jug of Leeds ware, 1810

233 Jug commemorating marriage of Queen Victoria, 1840

234 Jug with blue transfer decoration

234

233

235 Jug with painted Chinese style decoration, 1845

236 Measuring jug with official stamp, Birmingham

237 Mocha ware mug with chemical growth patterns, 1800

238 Mug decorated with sign language, 1825

239 Porcelain teapot made at Worcester

240 Porcelain teapot based on silver design, New Hall 1803

241 Teapot with rococo style decoration, Burslem 1843

242

242 Cadogan teapot filled through base
Spode 1825

243 Sheffield plate coffee pot with hot water jacket

244 Silver teapot

243

244

245 Coffee cup and saucer, Staffordshire 1840

246 Moustache cup and saucer, Minton 1840

247 Staffordshire plate with transfer design

248 Pottery plate from series entitled 'The Bottle'

249 Willow pattern plate

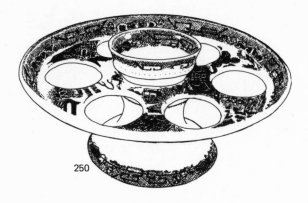

250 Willow pattern egg holder with salt, Spode 1830

251 Combined nightlight and milk warmer, Wedgwood 1810

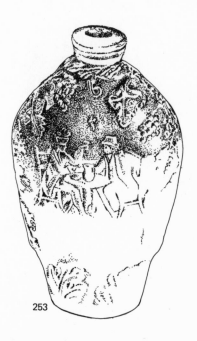

252 Rimmer's patent vapouriser, London

253 Stoneware spirit flask, 1840

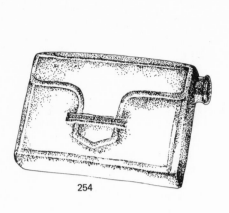

254

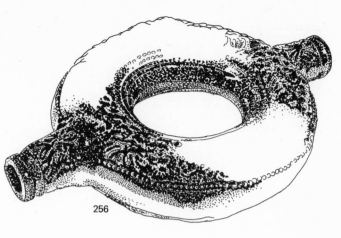

256

255a

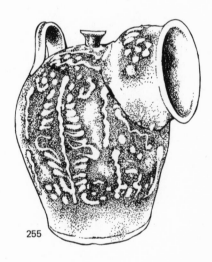

255

254 Stoneware spirit flask for pocket

255 Glazed slip ware salt jar made in Penrith

255a Earthenware 'Harvester's Bottle' for beer or cider

256 Water bottle carried on miner's arm

257 Earthenware hot water boot warmer

257

258 Pottery shapes for drying socks, Wedgwood

259 Baby's feeding bottle

259

260

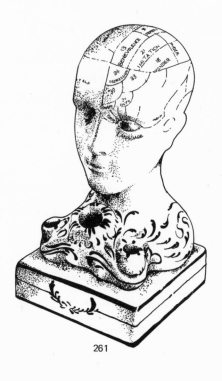

260 West Country jug with scratched graffito design, 1834

261 Phrenological head with inkwell base, 1835

261

262

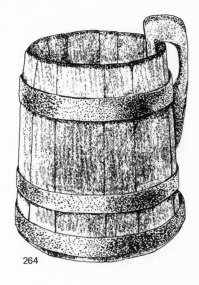

264

262 One pint pewter tankard

263 Wooden food bowl from Sussex

264 Wooden pail for dairy use

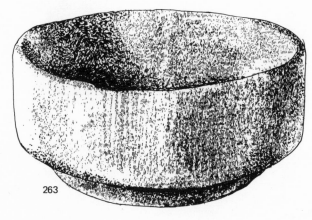

263

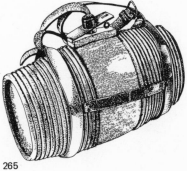

265 Wooden costrel or harvest barrel for cider

265

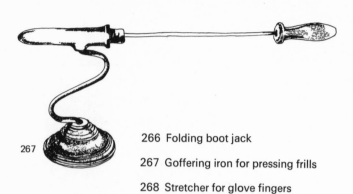

268

267

266

266 Folding boot jack

267 Goffering iron for pressing frills

268 Stretcher for glove fingers

269 Coconut shell goblet with silver mounts, 1841

270 Wooden potato masher

271 Boxwood lemon squeezer

272 Screw nutcracker in wood

273 Wooden ladle

269

270

271

272

273

274

275

274 Coffee or spice mill

275 Wooden biscuit mould

276 Workbasket for needlework

276

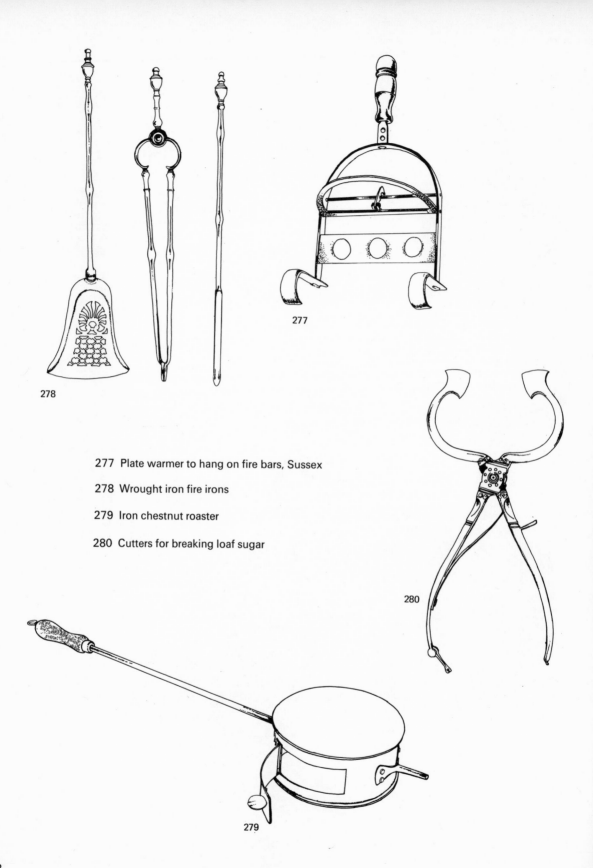

277 Plate warmer to hang on fire bars, Sussex

278 Wrought iron fire irons

279 Iron chestnut roaster

280 Cutters for breaking loaf sugar

281 Hot water foot warmer, copper

282 Egg whisk of tinned ironware

283 Meat fork

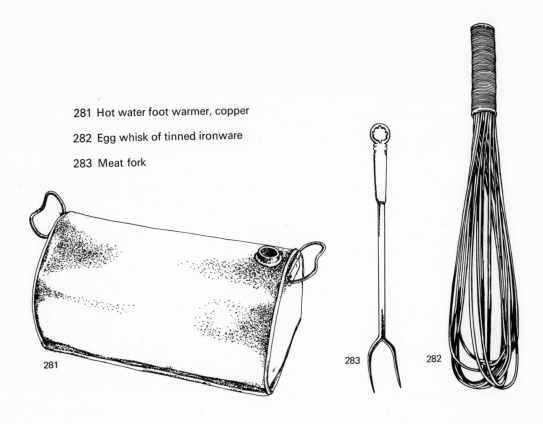

284 Copper bed warming pan with brass lid

285 Hot water stomach comforter

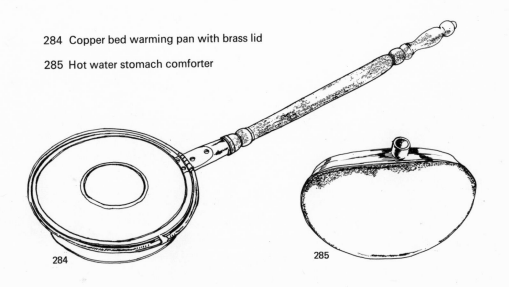

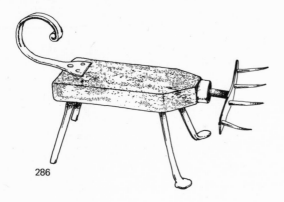

286 Wood and iron toasting dog

287a

287 Hanging girdle plate

287a Brass spoon and pastry jigger

288 Brass pan with wooden handle

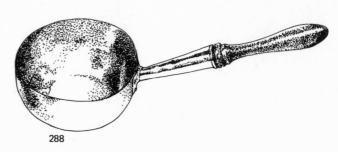

288

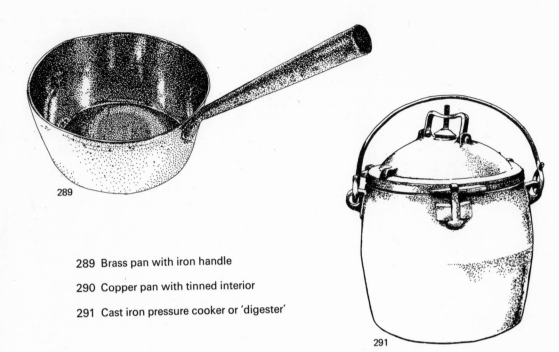

289

291

289 Brass pan with iron handle

290 Copper pan with tinned interior

291 Cast iron pressure cooker or 'digester'

290

292 Copper kettle

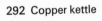

292

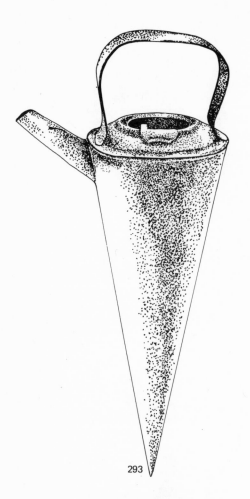

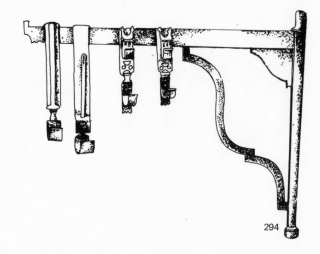

293 Conical kettle for pushing into fire

294 Iron chimney crane and pot hooks

295 Hinged pewter wheatsheaf butter mould

296 Copper jelly mould

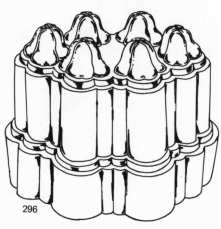

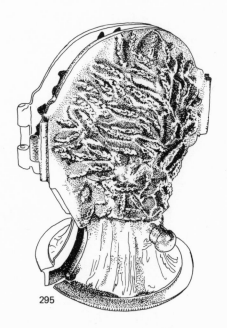

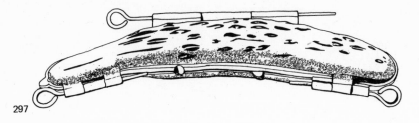

297 Pewter mould in shape of cucumber

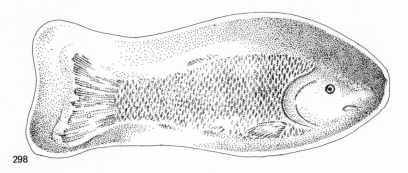

298 Earthenware mould for jellied fish

299 Box iron with opening for heater

300 Rotary fan bellows

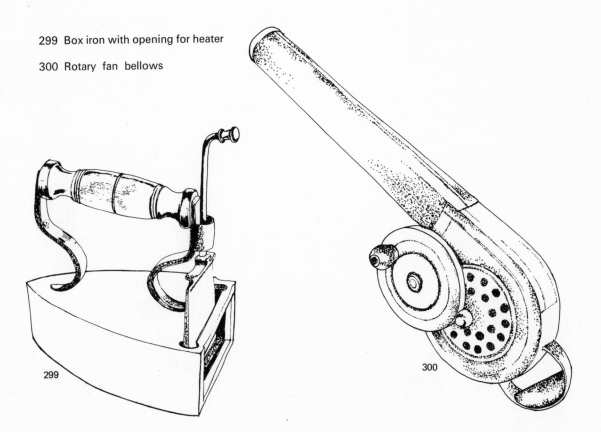

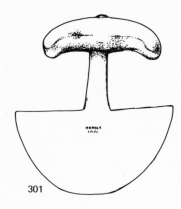

301

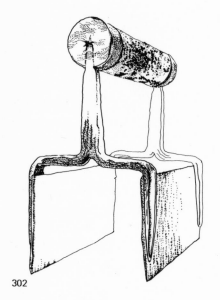

301 Meat choppers for use with bowl or board

302 Potato chopper

303 Copper colander

302

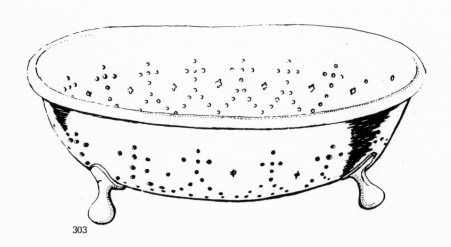

303

304

304 Tea caddy with curled paper decoration

305 Nailsea glass rolling pin

305

306 Glass ladle

307 Glass burnisher for starched linen

308 Blue glass ketchup bottle

306

307

308

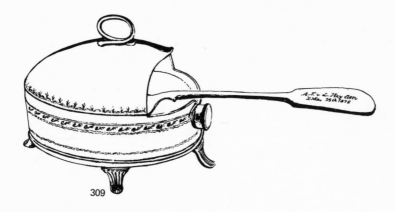

309 Sheffield plate spoon warmer

310 Silver salt cellar and sugar castor

311 Pepper pot of pewter and blue glass

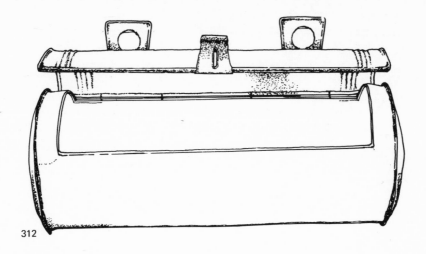

312 Candle box of black japanned iron

313 Pottery candle holder

314 Candle wick trimmer with box for trimmings

315 Phosphorus tipped matches or 'Congreves', 1845

316 Glass and silver spirit lamp

317 Office candlestick of French Empire style

317

318 Twin colza oil lamp with Argand burners

318

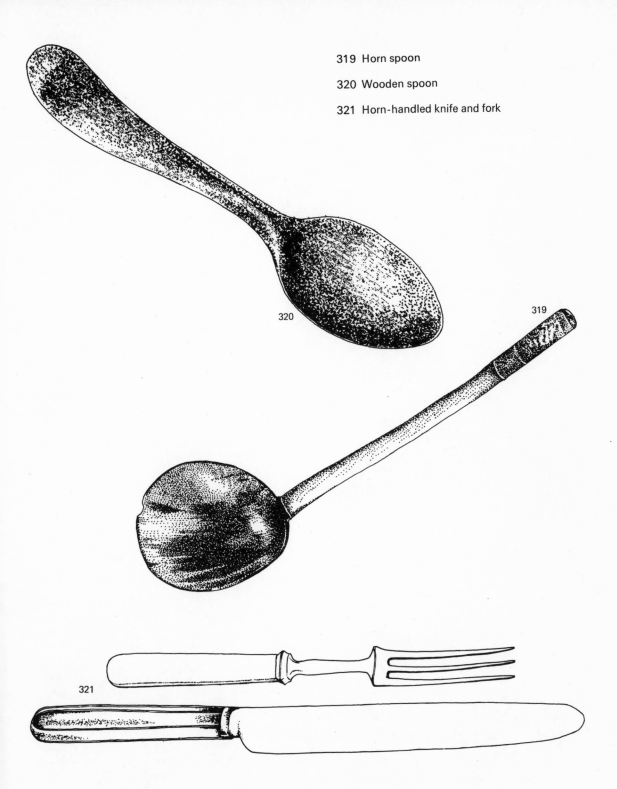

319 Horn spoon

320 Wooden spoon

321 Horn-handled knife and fork

320

319

321

Late Victorian 1850 – 1900

322

323

322 Water jug and hand bowl

323 Teacup and saucer, 1880

324 Tea cup and saucer with Chinese decoration

325 Moustache cup of grotesque design

324

325

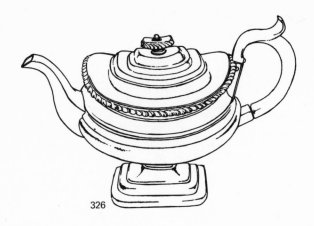

326

327

328

326 Silver plated teapot

327 Royle's patent self-pouring teapot in Brittania metal

328 Bone china teapot with chinoiserie decoration, 1870

329 Rockingham lustreware teapot

330 Copper tea kettle on spirit lamp stand

329

330

331 Rustic style sugar bowl, 1850

332 Staffordshire bone china sugar bowl, 1850

333 Large urn-shaped jug, 30 inches high

334 Highly decorated vase, 1890

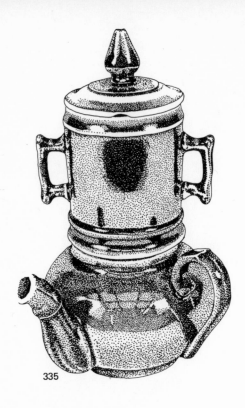

335

336

335 Brown glazed coffee percolator

336 Coffee percolator of tinplate

337 Coffee percolator of silver plate and copper

338 Wrought iron fire irons

337

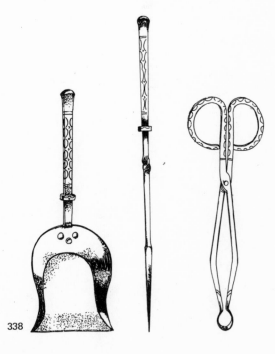

338

339 Brass jam pan

340 Cast-iron kettle

341 Cast-iron skillet

342 12 pint Devon harvest kettle of copper

343 Cast-iron kettle in shape of thatched cottage

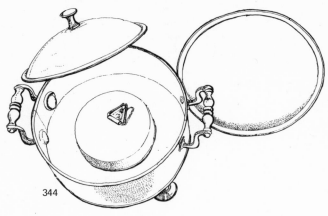

344

346

344 Cheese-melting dish from Lancashire

345 Brass trivet or 'footman'

346 Clockwork bottle jack, brass with grilling ring

345

347

348

347 Rotary gridiron with gravy cup

348 Fluted gridiron with gravy cup

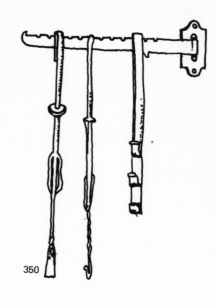

349 Dutch oven with clockwork bottle
jack

350 Jack rack for bottle jack

351 Toasting fork with heat shield

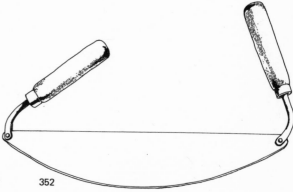

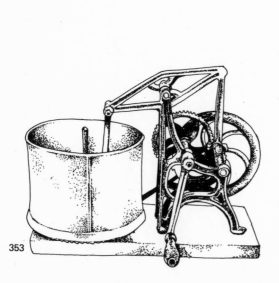

352 Herb chopper with hinged handles

353 Beam type chopping machine or mincer, 1890

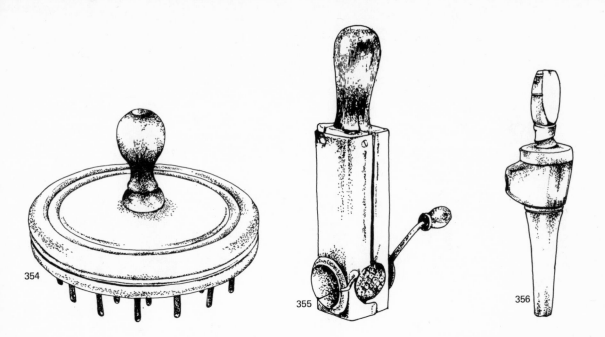

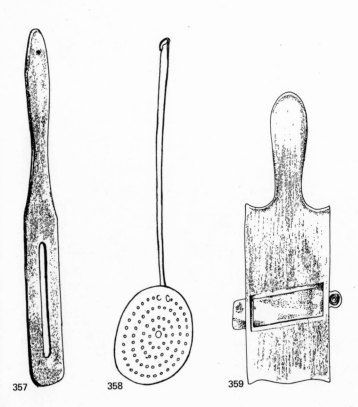

354 Wooden muffin pricker

355 Tinplate grater

356 Wooden tap for cider barrel

357 Wooden thible or porridge stirrer

358 Brass and iron skimmer

359 Wooden cucumber slice

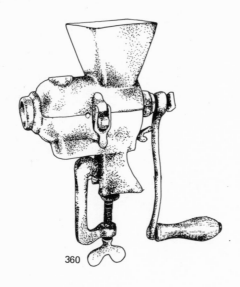

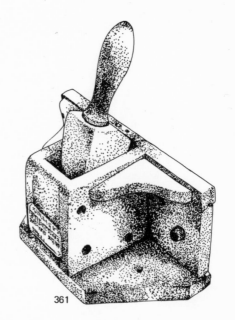

360 Cast-iron mincing machine

361 Wooden marmalade cutter

362 Nutcracker based on Mr. Punch

363 Self drawing corkscrew

364 Flour sieve of horsehair

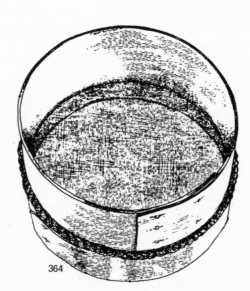

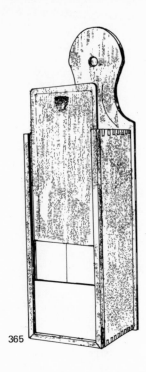

365

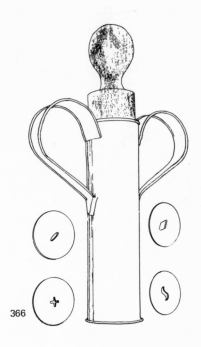

366

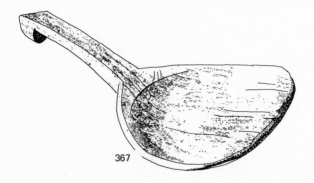

367

365 Wooden knife box

366 Icing sugar syringe of tinplate

367 Wooden cream skimmer

368 Wooden butter marker

369 Wooden butter curler

369

368

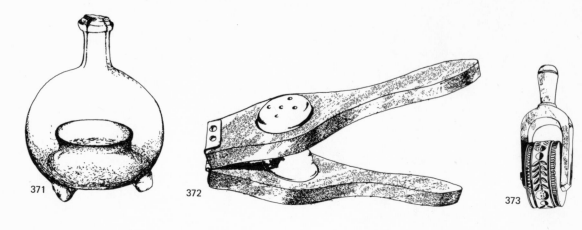

371 Wasp trap baited with beer or jam and water

372 Pottery and wood lemon squeezer

373 Roller type butter marker

374 Spice or nutmeg grater

375 Beadwork tea cosy

376 Wooden backboard to improve posture in girls' schools

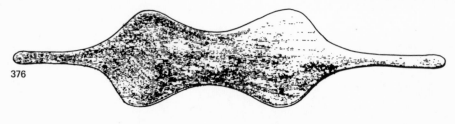

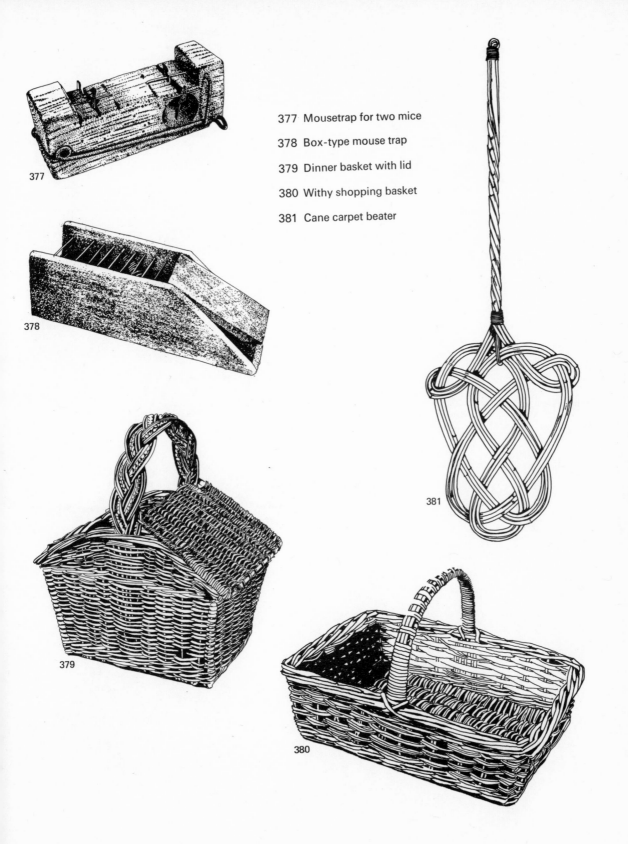

377 Mousetrap for two mice

378 Box-type mouse trap

379 Dinner basket with lid

380 Withy shopping basket

381 Cane carpet beater

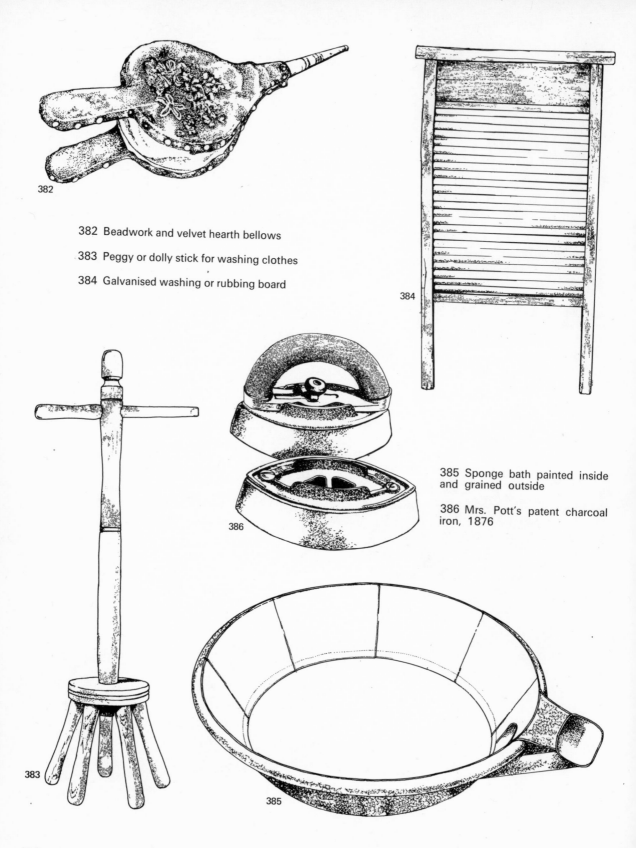

382 Beadwork and velvet hearth bellows

383 Peggy or dolly stick for washing clothes

384 Galvanised washing or rubbing board

385 Sponge bath painted inside and grained outside

386 Mrs. Pott's patent charcoal iron, 1876

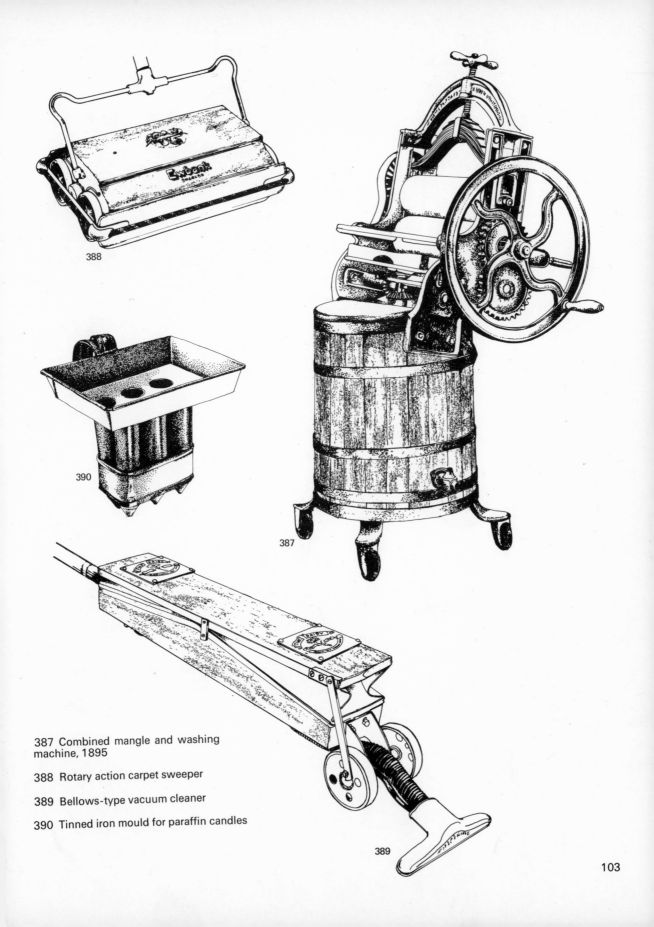

387 Combined mangle and washing
machine, 1895

388 Rotary action carpet sweeper

389 Bellows-type vacuum cleaner

390 Tinned iron mould for paraffin candles

392

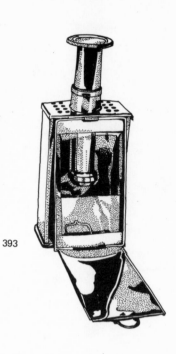

393

391

391 'Vauxhall' fairy light glass for candle

392 Wall candle sconce in painted tinplate

393 Two travellers' candle lamps

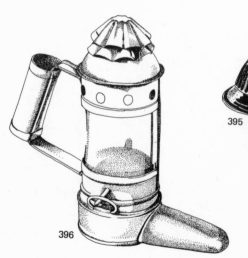

395

394

396

394 Cigar light matches

395 Brass spirit lamp

396 Oil lantern with shoe to fit in crevice

397 Pedestal lamp for paraffin oil

398 Elaborate brass watch stand

399 Ornate brass cotton reel stand

400

400 Writing set with ink-well
and taper holder

401 Earthenware hot water bottle

401

402

403

404

402 Pewter spoon

403 Tinplate cream ladle

404 Horn-handled knife

1900 – 1920

405

406

405 Wooden food box

406 Scottish cup reputedly made
from a donkey's knee

407 Wooden nutcrackers

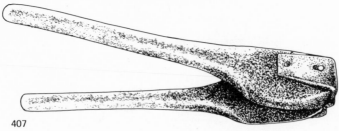

407

410

408 Wooden colander

409 Stoneware ginger beer bottle

410 Bellows for inflating air bed, 1912

408

409

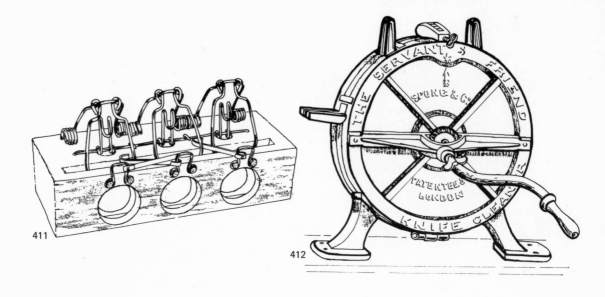

411

412

413

411 Irish-type three hole mousetrap

412 Rotary knife cleaner

413 Candle holder of wood

414 50 candlepower oil heater with ruby shade, 1914

415 150 candlepower paraffin oil heater, 1914

414

415

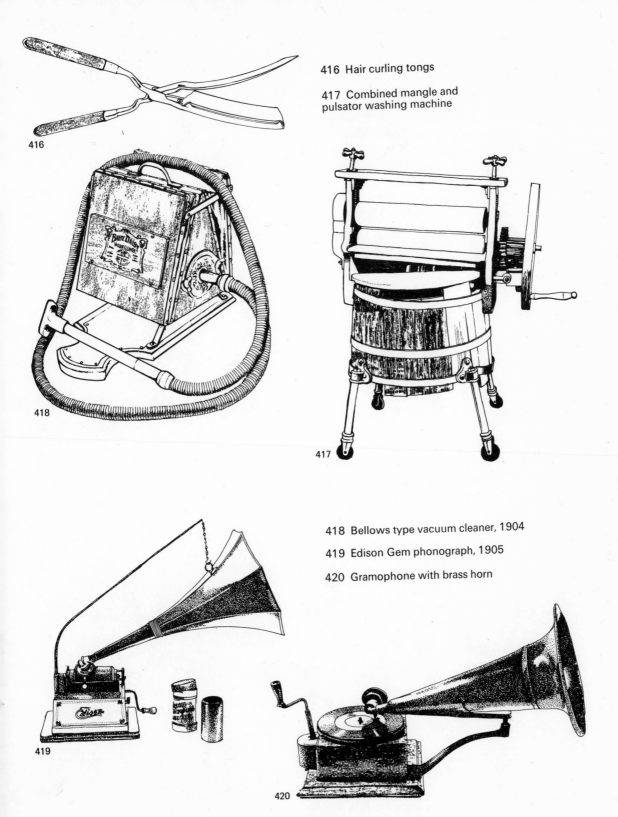

416 Hair curling tongs

417 Combined mangle and
pulsator washing machine

418 Bellows type vacuum cleaner, 1904

419 Edison Gem phonograph, 1905

420 Gramophone with brass horn

421

422

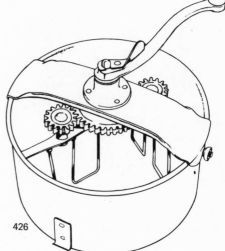

426

421 Tea can of blue enamelled iron

422 Cast-iron coffee or spice mill

423 Coffee or spice mill

424 Tinplate bread grater, 1901

425 Cast-iron mincing machine

426 Cake or bread mixer, 1908

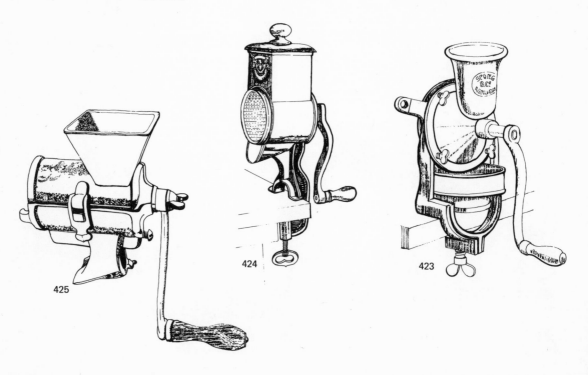

425

424

423

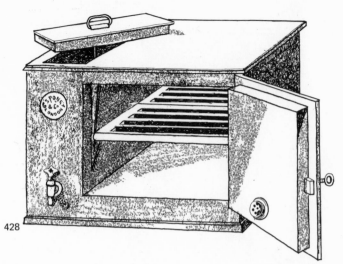

427 Ice refrigerator of wood, 1901

428 Zinc ice safe, 1901

430

429 Gas bracket light with candle effect, 1920

430 Painted glass gas light shades, 1920

431 Glass beaded gas light shades, 1910

429

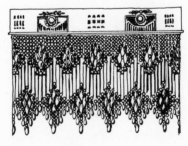

431

432

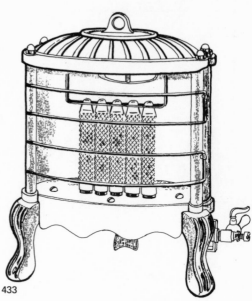

433

432 Kern gas radiator, 1920

433 Portable gas fire, 1920

434 Belling electric cooker, 1919

435 Electric cooker with tinplate utensils, 1919

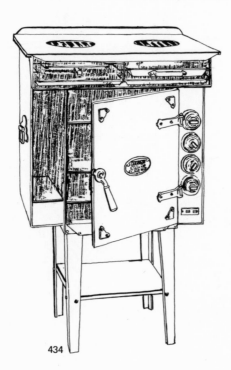

434

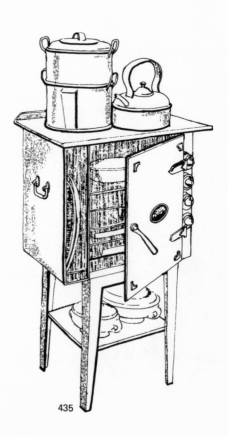

435

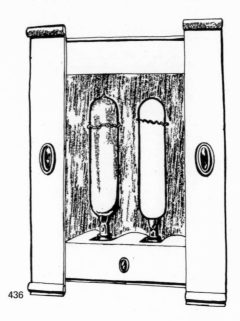

436

437

436 'Sausage lamp' electric heater

437 Electric fire with kettle warmer, 1912

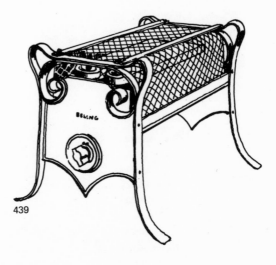

439

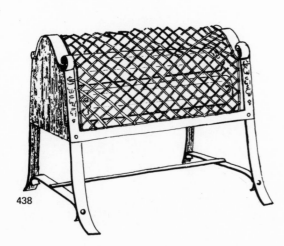

438

438 'Dainty' horizontal electric fire, 1914

439 Centre pattern electric fire, 1915

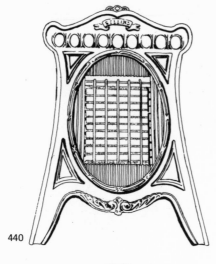

440

441

442

440 'Dainty' portable electric fire, 1919

441 Electric office fire, 1914

442 Boudoir electric fire, 1914

443 Concave electric dog-grate, 1915

444 'Sunflower' portable electric bowl fire

443

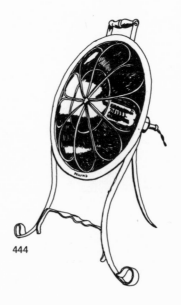

444

1920-1940

445

445 'Cut throat' razor and case

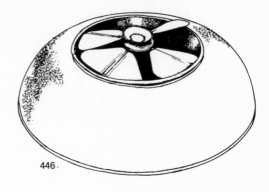

446

446 Cockroach and beetle trap

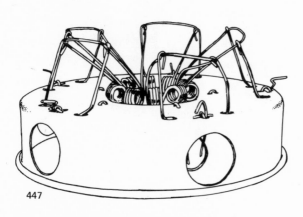

447

447 Tinplate trap to catch five mice

448

448 Sheet copper kettle

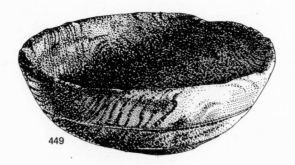

449

449 Elm bowl of traditional Berkshire pattern

450

450 Basketwork egg cup

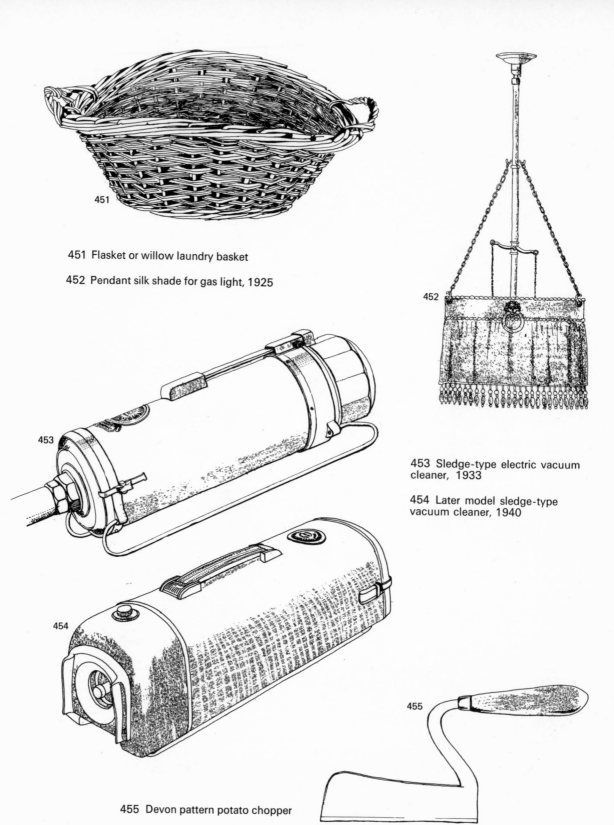

451 Flasket or willow laundry basket

452 Pendant silk shade for gas light, 1925

453 Sledge-type electric vacuum cleaner, 1933

454 Later model sledge-type vacuum cleaner, 1940

455 Devon pattern potato chopper

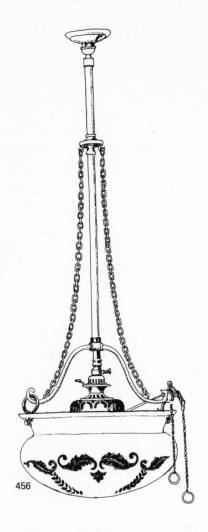

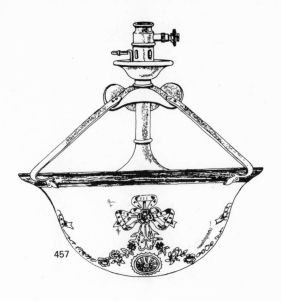

457 Etched glass bowl shade, 1930

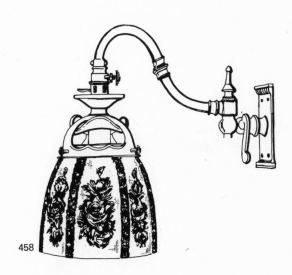

456 Bowl fitting gas light shade, 1925

458 Swing gas bracket, 1920

459 Etched and painted glass shades, 1925

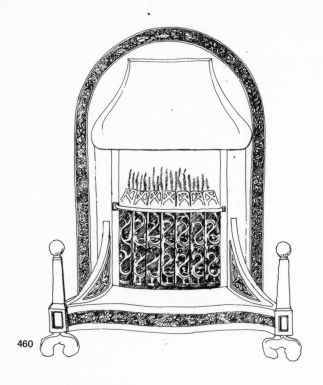

460

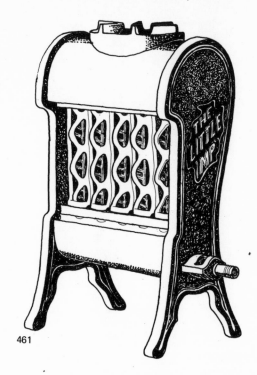

461

460 'Diomedes' dog-grate gas fire, 1928

461 Portable gas fire, 1928

462 Steamless gas radiator, 1928

463 Portable bowl-type gas fire, 1930

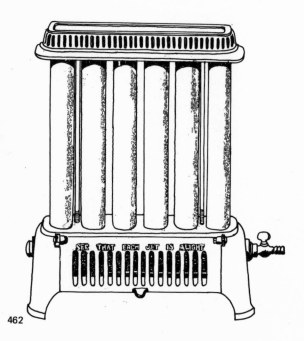

462

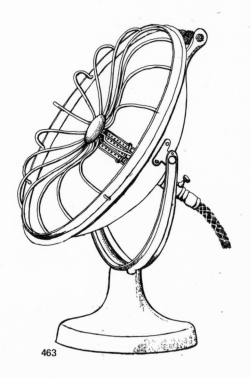

463

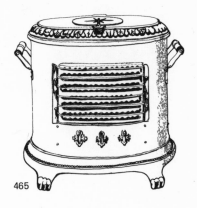

464

465

464 Gas fire 'fuel' bars, 1927

465 Electric fire with boiling ring, 1923

466 'Regal' electric fire, 1924

467 Utility electric fire, 1939

468 Turnbar electric fire, 1927

466

468

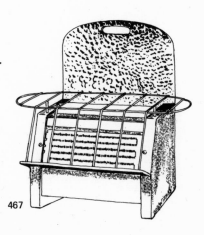

467

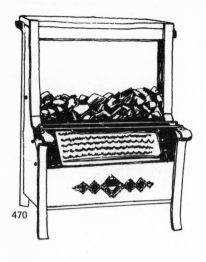

470

469

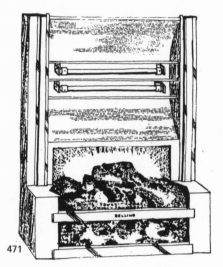

471

469 Electric fire with imitation coal fire effect, 1921

470 Electric fire with flicker coal effect, 1930

471 Reflector-type coal effect fire

472 Portable electric reflector fire, 1934

473 Belling cooker with aluminium utensils, 1926

472

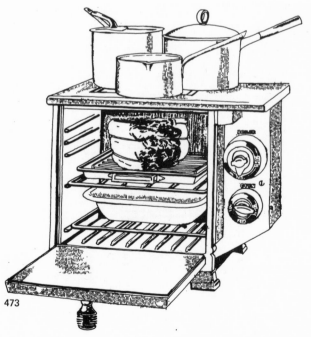

473

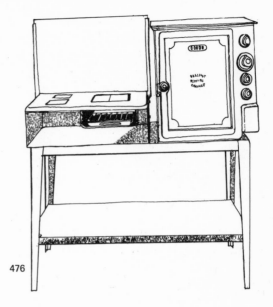

474 Advanced model electric cooker,1936

476 Electric cooker with side oven, 1926

475 Standard electric cooker, 1935

477 Early cabinet-style electric cooker, 1938

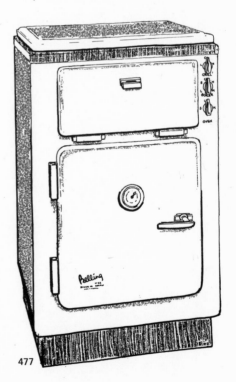

Index

Acorn knop 33
Adam, Robert 8, 9
Ale muller 52, 53
Amphora 17
Aquamanile 29
Argand lamp 88
Art Nouveau 11
Astbury ware 46

Baby's bottle 74
Backboard 100
Barbotine decoration 15, 17
Barrel tap 97
Baskerville, John 9
Basket 77, 101, 116
Bath 102
Beaker 15, 16, 17, 18, 19, 37, 65
Bed pan 54, 55
Bed warmer 39, 79
Beetle trap 115
Bellarmine 34
Bellows 83, 102, 107
Bermondes Delftware 36
Birmingham 68
Biscuit mould 77
Blackjack 37
Bolsover, Thomas 9
Boneware 22, 24, 32, 33
Boot jack 76
Boot warmer 73
Bottle 21, 34, 37, 64, 85, 107
Bottle jack 95
Bowl 17, 18, 23, 29, 30, 35, 47, 54, 75, 115
Bowyer of London 42
Box iron 83
Bread coaster 55
Bread grater 110
Brush 32
Burnisher 85
Burslem 69
Butter marker 99, 100
Butter mould 82

Cadogan 70
Candelabrum 61, 62
Candle box 87
Candle doughter 59
Candle mould 103
Candle snuffer 59, 87
Candlestick 21, 33, 38, 48, 60, 61, 62, 72, 87, 88, 104, 108

Caneware 46
Carpet beater 101
Carpet cleaner 103, 109, 116
Castor ware 17, 18
Cauldron, bronze 31
Chafing dish 57
Chamber pot 55
Charcoal iron 102
Charger 36
Cheam ware 26
Cheese coaster 55
Cheese dish 95
Chestnut roaster 78
Chimney crane 58, 82, 96
Chippendale, Thomas 8
Chocolate pot 40, 46, 63
Chopper 84 96, 116
Clay pipe 38
Clock 42
Coal helmet 53
Coaster 55
Coconut shell 51, 76
Coffee mill 77, 110
Coffee percolator 93
Coffee pot 40, 46, 63, 70
Colander 16, 84, 107
Comb, bone 24, 32
Comb, weaver's 24
Congreve matches 87
Cooker, electric 112, 120, 121
Corkscrew 98
Costrel 37, 73, 75
Council of Industrial Design 13
Cromwell 7
Crusie 59
Cucumber slice 97
Cup, silver 41

Dark Ages 5, 22–24
Decange of London 42
Derby 9, 67
Diamond knop 33
Digester 81
Dish slope 51
Dolly stick 102
Dolphin flask 21
Donkey's knee 107
Dutch oven 48, 96

Edwardian 11, 12, 106–115
Egg cup 50, 72, 115
Egg whisk 79

Elizabethan 7
Empire Exhibition 12
Enamel handle 43, 66
Ewer, bronze 31

Fan bellows 83
Festival of Britain 13
Fire irons 78, 93
Fishmongers' tankard 40
Fish mould 83
Flask 20, 21, 72, 73
Flesh hook 32
Flour sieve 98
Food box 49, 107
Food mixer 110
Fork 44, 66, 79, 89, 96
Frying pan 55

Gas shade 111, 116, 117
Ginger beer bottle 107
Girdle plate 80
Glassware 9, 20, 21, 64, 85
Glove powderer 49
Glove stretcher 76
Goblet 76
Goffering iron 76
Gothic 7, 10
Gramophone 109
Grater 97
Great Exhibition 7, 10
Great wheel 58
Grey Beard 34
Gridiron 56, 95

Hair curler 109
Hammerhead handle 44
Hancock, Joseph 9
Harvest kettle 94
Harvester's bottle 37, 73, 75
Heater, electric 113, 114, 119, 120
Heater, gas 112, 118
Hepplewhite, George 8
Hornware 43, 65, 66, 89
Horse-shoe handle 44
Hot-water bottle 79, 106

Ice safe 111
Industrial Revolution 8, 9
Ink well 106
Irons 83, 102
Italianate 7

Jacobean 6, 7, 34–44
Jar 17, 23, 73
Jasper ware 47
Jelly mould 82
Jones, Inigo 7
Jug 16, 19, 20, 25, 26, 28, 34, 45, 67, 68, 74, 90, 92

Kent, William 8
Ketchup bottle 85
Kettle 52, 81, 82, 91, 94, 112, 113, 115
Knife 22, 33, 43, 44, 66, 89, 106
Knife box 99
Knife cleaner 108

Ladle 49, 51, 76, 85, 106
Lambeth Delftware 35, 36
Lamp, colza 88
Lamp, gas 111, 116, 117
Lamp, oil 19, 20, 29, 59, 60, 104
Lamp, paraffin 105, 108
Lamp, spirit 87, 104
Lantern clock 42
Latten 29
Leatherware 37, 107
Ledeir of London 42
Leeds 46, 67
Lemon squeezer 51, 76, 100
Lethaby, William 12
Linen burnisher 85
Liverpool 45
London silver 41
Lowestoft 46

Maidenhead knop 33
Marmalade cutter 98
Match box 87, 104
Measure, pottery 27
Mediaeval 6, 25–33
Medicine spoon 65
Metropolitan slipware 35, 36
Mincer 84, 96, 98, 110
Miner's bottle 73
Minton 71
Mocha ware 68
Money box 50
Morris, William 11
Mortar 30
Mortarium 16
Mould 77, 82, 83
Mousetrap 58, 101, 108, 115
Moustache cup 71, 90

Muffin pricker 97
Mug 37, 45, 68
Multiple vase 15

Nailsea 10, 85
New Forest ware 15, 16
Nightlight 72
Nottingham 45
Nutcracker 76, 98, 107

Oven peel 57
Oven spade 57

Pail 75
Pan 30, 52, 53, 55, 80, 81, 94, 95
Papier mâché 9, 10
Pastry jigger 80
Peggy stick 102
Pepper pot 62, 86
Pewterware 39, 41, 44, 54, 55, 60, 75,
    82, 83
Phonograph 109
Phrenologist's head 74
Piggin 38, 50
Pipe rack 38
Pipkin 30, 35
Pitcher 25, 26, 27, 28
Plate 36, 39, 49, 54, 71
Plate tilter 51
Plate warmer 78
Platter 48, 49
Porridge stirrer 97
Porringer 35, 39, 49
Posset pot 36, 45
Potato masher 76
Pressure cooker 81
Pricket candlestick 33
Pugin, Augustus 10
Punch bowl 40
Puritan 7
Puritan stem 44

Razor 115
Reckan 58, 82, 96
Refrigerator 111
Regency 10, 67-72
Rimmer's vaporizer 72
Rockingham 91
Rococo 9, 10
Rolling pin 85
Rolls Royce 12
Romano British 5, 15-21
Royle's teapot 91
Rubbing board 102

Rushlight holder 38
Ruskin, John 10

Salt cellar 36, 63, 73, 86
Samian ware 5, 18
Sausage lamp 113
Scott, Walter 10
Shears 32
Sheraton, Thomas 8
Skewer 22
Skillet 20, 31, 48, 52, 94
Skimmer 97, 99
Sock dryer 74
Spice box 50
Spice grater 100
Spice mill 77, 110
Spinning wheel 58
Spode 70, 72
Spoon 22, 24, 33, 44, 65, 66, 80, 89,
    106
Spoon warmer 86
Stafford 45, 47, 71, 92
Stomach comforter 79
Strainer 16
Strike-a-light 60, 62
Sugar bowl 92
Sugar castor 86
Sugar cutter 78
Sugar icer 99
Sunderland 47

Table clock 42
Tankard 40, 45, 75
Tea caddy 63, 85
Tea can 110
Tea cosy 100
Teacup 47, 71, 90
Teapot 46, 69, 70, 91
Tear bottle 21
Terra sigillata 5, 18
Thible 97
Thread stand 105
Toaster 56, 80, 96
Traveller's lamp 104
Treen 24, 30, 37, 38, 40, 48, 49, 50,
    51, 58, 75, 76, 77, 89, 97, 98, 99,
    100, 101, 106, 107, 108, 115
Trefoil handle 44
Trencher 48, 49
Trivet 57, 95
Tudor 6, 7, 34-44
Turner 46
Tyg 36, 45

Unguent bottle 21
Urn 63

Vanbrugh, John 8
Vapourizer 72
Vase 15, 67, 92
Vauxhall light 104
Vegetable slice 97, 98
Victorian 10, 11, 12, 67–105

Waffle iron 56
Washing board 102
Washing machine 103, 109

Wasp trap 100
Watch stand 105
Weaver's comb 24
Wedgwood, Josiah 9, 47, 72, 74
Wick trimmer 59, 87
Wig stand 51
Wine bottle 21, 34, 37, 64
Wine glass 64
Worcester 9, 45, 46, 47, 69
Wren, Christopher 8
Writhen knop 33
Writing set 106

York silver 41

2012
9
√ ευ νλες
√ Λ∂ε